For the Liberty of Ireland at Home and Abroad

✦

CLASSICS OF IRISH HISTORY
General Editor: Tom Garvin

Some recent titles
Original publication dates of reprinted titles are given in brackets

For the Liberty of Ireland at Home and Abroad

The Autobiography of J. F. X. O'Brien

✴

J. F. X. O'BRIEN

edited by
Jennifer Regan-Lefebvre

UNIVERSITY COLLEGE DUBLIN PRESS
Preas Choláiste Ollscoile Bhaile Átha Cliath

In memory of
Mary Jayne Regan, Marilyn Murray Waywood and Richard Regan

First published by
University College Dublin Press, 2010

ISBN 978–1–904558–99–6
ISSN 1393–6883

University College Dublin Press
Newman House, 86 St Stephen's Green
Dublin 2, Ireland
www.ucdpress.ie

Cataloguing in Publication data available
from the British Library

Typeset in Scotland in Ehrhardt by Ryan Shiels
Text design by Lyn Davies, Frome, Somerset, England
Printed in England on acid-free paper by
CPI Antony Rowe, Chippenham

CONTENTS

A Note on the Text

O'Brien's untitled autobiography was handwritten in instalments between 1895 and 1898 and is held as a manuscript in the National Library of Ireland. O'Brien asked his close friend and colleague, Alfred Webb, to read and comment on the text. Webb was an experienced writer and editor and he made extensive comments. Their correspondence seems to indicate that O'Brien was prepared to make many of the changes that Webb suggested.

In some cases it is impossible to tell whether notes on the text were made by Webb, by O'Brien himself, or by a third party. I have made a decision in good faith to incorporate changes where they correct grammar, delete repetitions, or generally make the text more readable, or, regarding content, where there is some indication that O'Brien approved the changes. I have not touched O'Brien's inconsistent personal name spelling where I have been unable to trace the person. As noted in the text, I have excluded one chapter (concerning an O'Brien family holiday to France), due to space limitations.

There is also an undated, typed version of the autobiography held in the National Library of Ireland. It is not clear when this was produced; one possibility is that it was typed by one of O'Brien's children after his death. I have not transcribed from this copy, but from the original, though in fact my version turned out to be nearly identical to the typed copy.

O'Brien's correspondence indicates that he wrote the text with the intention of publishing it for a broad audience. The text has not, to my knowledge, ever been published in full, although selections were published by Pat McCarthy in the journal *Decies*.[1]

---

1   Pat McCarthy, 'James Francis Xavier O'Brien (1828–1905): Dungarvan-born fenian', *Decies: The Journal of the Waterford Archaeological and Historical Society*, 54 (1998).

ACKNOWLEDGEMENTS

I would like to thank the Keeper of Manuscripts of the National Library of Ireland for permission to publish Manuscript 16,695. It is always a pleasure to work at the National Library and I would particularly like to thank Kieran McGee, who took a real interest in the project and whose curiosity and enthusiasm were much appreciated. I would also like to thank the staff of the libraries of Queen's University Belfast and the Centre Culturel Irlandais in Paris, where additional research was carried out. Anne Lenihan of the Waterford County Library kindly tracked down a hard-to-find article. I thank the Library of Congress for providing the cover image. I thank the Waterford County Museum (www.waterford countyimages.org) for permission to use the portrait of O'Brien for the back cover, and to Michael Fitzgerald for his assistance in obtaining a copy of the image.

A version of my introduction was presented at the Centre for History and Economics seminar at the University of Cambridge, and I thank the participants for their feedback. Thanks also to James McConnel and Matthew Kelly for their encouragement and suggestions at the early stages of the project.

I thank my colleagues at Queen's University Belfast and the University of Exeter for their support and encouragement. In particular, I am grateful to Patrick Maume, Colin Reid, Caoimhe Nic Dháibhéid, Anthony Stanonis for sharing his knowledge of the history of New Orleans, Patrick McCafferty for helping me to trace Irish meteorological events, and Duncan Redford and Laura Rowe for answering my questions about

For the Liberty of Ireland

nineteenth-century maritime history. Students in my Decolonisation in Ireland class in Exeter have pushed me to think harder about Fenianism, and the book is better for it.

Barbara Mennell supported this project from the beginning. She and Noelle Moran were much more patient editors than I deserved. My parents and husband were a constant support. The dedication is to the memory of my grandparents, three individuals who are sorely missed and strongly associated with my progress as a student of Irish history.

INTRODUCTION
Jennifer Regan-Lefebvre

James Francis Xavier O'Brien (1829?–1906) is best known for being an insurrectionist, political prisoner and member of the Irish Parliamentary Party in the 1880s and 1890s, but his autobiography reveals a life of adventure and bohemian travel before he embraced organised nationalism. O'Brien's autobiography provides both detailed observations of social and economic history and fanciful accounts of his own motivations and historical role. Up until his imprisonment in 1867, O'Brien's life is presented as a search for adventure and a jubilant witness to romantic Irish nationalism. His story then segues into his experiences as a political prisoner and his journey into constitutional Irish nationalism.

O'Brien wrote his autobiography in the late 1890s, and as will be explored below, the ways in which he chose to present his life reflect the debates and tensions in Irish politics at that time. A brief overview of O'Brien's life will provide a neutral starting point. O'Brien was born between 1829 and 1831 into a large, comfortably-off Catholic merchant family in Dungarvan, County Waterford. O'Brien was educated by private tutors, then decided to enter a seminary in 1848. At a young age he was exposed to the ideas of Father Mathew, a temperance advocate, and Daniel O'Connell's non-violent Repeal movement, but also showed interest in military force to achieve Irish national independence. His religious studies were interrupted by James Fintan Lalor's small insurrection in Cappoquin, County Waterford in 1849. The police sought O'Brien in connection with the insurrection, but he evaded arrest by fleeing to England. On his return, he worked in the family business, then

in 1854 matriculated to Queen's College, Galway, to study medicine. He
spent a year studying abroad in Paris. In 1856 he decided to sail to
Nicaragua to fight for the American filibusterer William Walker. This
adventure ended abruptly with Walker's surrender, and O'Brien settled
in Louisiana and worked as a schoolteacher and bookkeeper. When the
American Civil War broke out he joined a regiment in the Confederacy
but did not experience battle. He left New Orleans with his first wife and
two children in 1862 and returned to Ireland, where he worked as a book-
keeper and became more involved in the Irish Republican Brotherhood,
or Fenian, movement. Fenians were republicans who advocated armed
rebellion to obtain Irish independence from Great Britain. He took part
in the 1867 Fenian Rising and was caught and arrested as a leader.
O'Brien was tried and convicted of high treason for his involvement – a
charge that, at the time, carried the sentence of being hung, drawn and
quartered. This sentence was commuted to one of life imprisonment
with penal servitude, and that in turn was amnestied in 1869. O'Brien
kept a relatively low public profile in the 1870s. He became convinced by
the electoral promise of the Irish Parliamentary Party, which was
progressing towards legislation for devolved Irish government. He was
elected an MP for this party in the election of 1885 and remained an MP
until his death in 1905. He joined the majority of Irish MPs in opposing
Charles Stewart Parnell's leadership during the split of 1890–1. As an
MP, he was 'precariously neutral' and undistinguished, but he served
the Party and its affiliate organisations in Britain as a competent book-
keeper and treasurer.[1]

O'Brien's story is useful (and entertaining) for two reasons. First, he
provides detailed accounts of his experiences as a Fenian, particularly as
a prisoner, and these accounts have already informed the histories of the
Irish Republican Brotherhood movement and of nineteenth-century
Irish nationalism in general.[2] Less emphasised in the existing historio-
graphy, his itinerant youth makes him an unlikely, and fascinating,
character in world history. In the 1850s O'Brien travelled through France,
the Caribbean, Latin America, and the American South. The ease with
which he travelled, his return migration from the United States, and his
participation in several major politico-military campaigns were all

remarkable for an Irishman of his time, but what is most striking is how little impact these travels appear to have made on his interests, outlook and worldview. On Latin America and the Caribbean in particular, there is an extensive European travel writing from the first half of the nineteenth century, and a correspondingly broad scholarly treatment of this literature that has emphasised themes of imagined conquest and transformative inter-cultural encounters in 'contact zones'.[3] O'Brien's writing does not fit neatly into this canon. Rather, he presents his interest as narrowly focused on Irish nationalism, and he was able to maintain this focus because he moved amongst the Irish diaspora in France, the United States and Britain. He claims to have been a born adventurer, yet displayed a remarkable lack of curiosity: about the cultures he encountered, the context of the campaigns in which he took part, and even his own date of birth. O'Brien was a revolutionary but a social conservative, and a person of uncommonly broad education for his time, but one who either did not favour deep reflection, or who selectively remembered and recorded his past to present a particular moral message.

O'Brien may have simply forgotten details of his earlier travels that would have coloured his account differently. Writing his autobiography in the late 1890s, when he was an MP in a troubled Irish Parliamentary Party, charged with the unenviable task of managing its strained finances, he struggles with his own memory for names and events. He balances this with description of the natural world around him and the physical attributes of the people he encounters. The text is not remarkable for its literary style: the prose is sometimes clumsy and the narrative disorganised or repetitive. As with any biographical account we must recognise how the passage of time shapes an individual's recollection of earlier events, and of how subsequent public remembrance of those events can even modify the memories of first-hand witnesses and participants. O'Brien's memoir is not simply an account of his earlier political activity: it is a reflection of the Irish political climate in which he was writing at the end of the nineteenth century.

Previous historical writing about O'Brien has portrayed him as an unsung Irish hero; in introducing the text of his memoir, this editor neither wishes to celebrate nor condemn O'Brien's political choices, but the editorial role compels me to comment on the structure of the text, its consistency and accuracy, and its strengths and limitations as a historical source. Had O'Brien published the work during his lifetime, and he indicated that he intended to, he may have become one of the 'patriarchal figures' through whose memoirs the Irish public's impressions of Fenianism were shaped.[4] Perhaps to bolster Irish nationalism when he felt it was endangered, or in an attempt to rescue his own reputation from accusations that he had betrayed the Fenian ideal by becoming an MP, O'Brien has carefully presented his life as a narrative of sole and pure dedication to Irish nationalism. He represents himself as hard-working, devoutly Catholic, self-sacrificing, sober, and righteous, even stressing his naïveté when confronted with immoral behaviour and drunkenness. He admits no political mistakes, but situates himself as the voice of reason and morality when others were exercising poor judgement, whether at student parties in Galway in 1854, in the Fenian Rising of 1867, or socialising with English politicians in 1895. We can only speculate as to what other kind of reflection he might have provided he had not been so clearly concerned with maintaining this narrative, even when it seems improbable given the evidence he has provided about his life. Living, for example, in cosmopolitan Paris in the 1850s, O'Brien does not portray himself as influenced by Parisian republicanism, enthused by the political atmosphere of the multinational community, or affected by the experience of leaving rural Leinster for a dynamic global capital. He may have been protecting himself from popular associations of Paris as a bohemian, republican (in the sense of being anti-Catholic) and generally decadent city.

There is an innocence in O'Brien's description of his trajectory, like an Irish Candide without the biting social critique of a Voltaire. He did have the assistance of a skilled editor, Alfred Webb. Webb and O'Brien were both MPs – Webb represented O'Brien's home constituency of West Waterford 1890–5 – and shared treasury duties for the various organs of Irish constitutional nationalism.[5] The two shared a voluminous correspondence, now held in the National Library of Ireland, and Webb also made copious notes on O'Brien's draft memoir, referring to it as 'a labour of love'.[6] These notes have been preserved in the text, as they reveal a close friendship that overcame deep ideological differences: years before they met, Webb was campaigning for the abolition of American slavery just as O'Brien was fighting for the American Confederacy. There is also the possibility that had the two worked further on editing the memoir a more reflective O'Brien would have emerged.

O'Brien has divided his text into ten chronological chapters. He begins Chapter One by describing his upbringing in a privileged merchant family with a strong sense of its own ancient role in shaping Irish history. Although his was a common Irish surname (his mother was also born an O'Brien, and his first wife was the widow of a man named O'Brien), O'Brien believed that he descended from a branch of the O'Brien Gaelic ruling dynasty of Thomond, County Clare that had migrated to Waterford in the fourteenth century. He describes his desire to fight for Irish independence as stemming from the fact 'that I had in my veins the blood of an old, illustrious race'. The family's middle–class circumstances meant that he grew up in a household with servants, was educated privately, had access to reading material, and had guaranteed employment in the family business when he was not attending university, enrolled in seminary, or travelling.

O'Brien names his early influences as Catholic priests, the temperance campaigner Father Mathew, Daniel O'Connell and his political Repeal movement, and Irish mythology and nationalistic children's literature. He became acquainted with a number of future Fenians through family and personal connections in the Waterford area, and his older brother, Christopher O'Brien, belonged to the local Repeal Club.[7] O'Connell's reputation is largely upheld in O'Brien's hands: though O'Brien deeply regretted that physical force had been a mere negotiating bluff on O'Connell's part, he remains laudatory of O'Connell's overall political achievements.

O'Brien explains that he was anxious to fight for Ireland but that, after the disappointing failure of the 1848 Young Ireland rebellion, he decided instead to enter a seminary to become a Catholic priest. A skirmish in 1849 led by James Fintan Lalor at Cappoquin, Waterford, was O'Brien's first involvement in seditious activity, although the real unsung hero in his text seems to have been a Miss Hickey, who concealed weapons in a handbasket. O'Brien came under suspicion with the police, and was able to use his family trade connections to abscond to south Wales, where he toured the English coast until it was deemed safe to return: in effect, he took an unplanned holiday in the very country against which he had been planning treasonous activities.

Rounding out this story of a model nationalist upbringing, O'Brien describes in vivid detail the Irish Famine, in which he paints a picture of himself as a sad observer of British cruelty. O'Brien writes that the British government preferred to allow peasants to starve than to see landlords' rents unpaid, whereas an Irish government would have fought for the peoples' welfare. Arguing that 'not even the Sultan of Turkey would surely help to export the food of his people while famine raged among them', a popular comparison in which the Sultan symbolised foreign despotism (and, paradoxically, perhaps a reference to the Sultan's generous £1,000 donation to Irish famine relief in 1847[8]), O'Brien lays this charge on the government: 'While our country was thus desolated, as many as 20 or more carts each laden with about a ton of wheat, oats, etc. would come from inland towns escorted by military and police.' O'Brien is thus presenting a classic nationalist narrative of the Famine – that the very food being exported could have prevented mass starvation, and that the government bore sole responsibility for not interfering with this trade – which most scholars now recognise as oversimplified.[9] But regardless of the limitations in O'Brien's historical interpretation, there is a major contradiction in his storytelling, one that calls into question his reflections and analysis. He notes several times, only a few pages later, that from 1847 to 1853 he was working in the O'Brien family business, 'buying oats and butter for shipment to England'. O'Brien's displacement from his own involvement may be an extension of his belief that Britain alone was culpable for the trauma of the Famine, or, paradoxically, it could suggest latent feelings of guilt and responsibility.

Chapter Two describes how, in 1854, O'Brien attended Queen's College Galway (later known as University College Galway and, currently, the National University of Ireland, Galway), founded in 1845 along with sister institutions in Belfast and Cork. Designed to be inoffensively non-denominational, the colleges were instead derided as 'godless' institutions, and Catholic clergy discouraged their faithful from attending. In the text O'Brien criticises his friend John O'Leary sharply for making a public statement that he would flout this prohibition; although not clear from his writing, O'Brien must be rebuking O'Leary's decision to make a public statement or to have attended without clerical permission, not his decision to attend one of the colleges. O'Brien's description of his time in Galway emphasises how he tried to follow a righteous and moral path, embodying the self-reliance and self-control emphasised by the Mathewite temperance movement. He contrasts this with the behaviour of others around him: a priest who treats penitents in the confessional and children harshly, drunken and disorderly peers, and a college professor who condemns patriotic song and, O'Brien asserts, denied him a prize based on his political beliefs.

After a year in Galway O'Brien moved to Paris to pursue his medical studies (he claims that this was a mistake, but never explains precisely why). His decision to move to Paris seems partly to have been inspired by the strong reputation of the medical tuition, and partly by his admiration for brothers John and Arthur O'Leary. He does not seem to have socialised with James Stephens and John O'Mahony, future Fenians who lived in Paris from 1849 to 1855, and were therefore leaving Paris as O'Brien was arriving. Nor does O'Brien seem to have had the same politically forma-tive experience that Stephens's biographer describes in his Parisian sojourn, arguing that 'the advanced student circles at the Sorbonne may have played a role in this phase of Stephens's political education; the same may be said of the Irish exile community. The Irish College itself, O'Mahony's workplace, was a reputed hotbed of republicanism during the 1850s.'[10] O'Brien socialised with other Irish nationalist expatriates, including O'Leary, John Martin, Kevin Izod O'Doherty, and Eva O'Kelly O'Doherty, famed for her poetry in the Young Ireland newspaper and literary magazine, *The Nation*.

These Irish expatriates also befriended a young American artist, James MacNeill Whistler. Whistler has been described as 'ahead of the crowd of expatriates,' moving to Paris in 1855; larger number of foreign artists arrived after the 1880s.[11] Whistler's model and mistress, Jo Heffernan, was also Irish, so evidently he enjoyed the Irish company he found in Paris.[12] Commenting on the experience of Scottish migrants to Paris, Siân Reynolds has observed that 'when students arrived in Paris, they were not really going into a French milieu so much as a cosmopolitan one'.[13] O'Brien, living though he was in the heart of the Latin Quarter of Paris and socialising with a man who would be one of the major artists of fin-de-siècle Europe, seems something of an accidental cosmopolitan, one who did not seek out or revel in the diversity of Paris; again, perhaps he is merely distancing himself from the reputed degeneracy of the city. According to his memoir, he had one goal: to seek out opportunities that would help him to orchestrate Irish political independence.

In Chapter Three, after a break from medical studies due to illness, O'Brien decided that domestic opportunities to liberate Ireland were lacking, and in 1856, set sail to Nicaragua to earn military experience. Nicaragua had gained independence from Spain in 1821. The Central American country provided a land-and-sea route from the Atlantic to Pacific oceans and both the United States and Britain realised its strategic potential; the Clayton-Bulwer Treaty of 1850 declared that both states had an interest but neither had a right to annex Nicaragua. Plans were already underway to construct a canal across Nicaragua; it would never be realised, and ultimately the route was constructed through Panama.[14] British-American imperial competition in the region was layered on top of major rivalries between indigenous liberals and conservatives – rivalries that were particularly intense in Nicaragua. In 1855 an American filibusterer, William Walker, led a military insurgency into Nicaragua to support the liberals, became head of the army and then president. He envisioned an extension of the mentalities and economies of the Southern American states into Latin America, complete with slavery and plantations. Faced with a conservative opposition from surrounding states, he surrendered on 1 May 1857 and was evacuated with American assistance.[15]

O'Brien went to Nicaragua to fight for Walker, whose progress through the region had been reported in Irish newspapers: the Dublin *Freeman's Journal* (then a liberal-nationalist publication) reported in April 1856 that 'the common impression, among those who have traced the progress of affairs most carefully, is that the effeminate half-breeds of Costa Rica can offer no effectual resistance to the well-trained desperate followers of "The Great Filibuster".[16] In contrast, the conservative *Belfast News-letter* quoted an American senator calling Walker a 'ruffian buccaneer and pirate'.[17] Evidently, Walker was viewed through the lens of Irish domestic politics, and as well as the promise of exciting battle, O'Brien may have relished the opportunity to fight, in effect, against Britain's interests. Victory for Walker would have strengthened American influence in the region and, in a zero-sum regional political game, correspondingly weakened British influence, and may have eventually even destabilised British control over its Caribbean colonies.

Ironically, battle eluded O'Brien (Walker surrendered first), but he found himself taking refuge in the British Consul's home after a bar brawl, an act which he found deeply humiliating. The failure of Walker's expedition led O'Brien to New Orleans, though he had considered instead going to Calcutta; evidently he felt that his opportunities for travel were unlimited. He was encountering exciting new things on his travels, like mosquito netting and rocking chairs, and had swum in shark-infested Caribbean waters. Along his travels he admired the beauty of the flora and fauna but believed that the lush, dense vegetation of Nicaragua was uninhabited, and that its overgrowth was evidence of neglect and want of industrious civilisation.

In Chapter Four, he describes the booming port city at the mouth of the Mississippi: the excitement of paddle boat races, the levees that protected the city from the Gulf of Mexico, and the more relaxed social codes and seepage of domestic life onto the public streets through verandas and porches. O'Brien believed that climate was partly to blame for the different attitudes he encountered, as 'the people of warm latitudes are naturally much warmer in their feelings and temperaments than those in higher latitudes; this is recognised all the world over, and accordingly is taken with consideration when judging their actions'.

Antebellum New Orleans boasted a vibrant cultural mix of recent immigrants from Europe and established communities from France and Africa (although he makes no reference to the latter community, New Orleans had a significant free black population as well as slaves). O'Brien took for granted the unofficial ethnic segregation of the city, which seemed natural enough for him as he used (exclusively) the Irish community to secure himself lodging, friends, a wife, and eventually employment in a Jesuit school in Baton Rouge. Although he was now a French speaker, O'Brien does not suggest that the language enabled him to progress professionally or socially in Louisiana.

O'Brien's reflections on the system of slavery are uncomfortable to the modern reader, as well as they were to his abolitionist friend Webb. Though he admits that slavery was not a defensible system, he argues that critiques were 'grossly exaggerated' and hypocritical on the part of Northerners who, in a previous century, had owned slaves. He was repulsed by his first personal encounter with a slave. O'Brien had great confidence in his powers of observation and, after having observed some slaves on the way to church, extrapolated that slaves were generally well treated, the atmosphere of plantations 'was of the most genial and friendly character', and yet most slaves were child-like in nature and intellect and thus benefited from the paternalism of a slave master. This infantilised view of non-white people was not unusual in nineteenth-century Britain; it informed the civilising mission of British imperialism and can be found expressed in very similar language, for example, in advice to British women on dealing with Indian domestic servants.[18]

Victorians used the term 'race' where modern thinkers would often prefer 'ethnicity'. O'Brien saw Irish people as a unique race, and he was surprised that Central Americans did not appreciate the same racial distinctions as he did, commenting that he met, 'specimens of probably every race of white men on the earth – but in Nicaragua they were [all] known as Americanos.' Nineteenth-century Irish attitudes towards non-white 'races' were flexible and racial language was often used as a metaphorical strategy to parallel nationalist positions.[19] Irish nationalist idiom sometimes stressed solidarity with enslaved or oppressed people; this could be for larger humanitarian purposes, as in the writing of Alfred Webb or Michael Davitt, or merely a rhetorical device. Alternatively, John Mitchel, the Irish nationalist who settled in the American South, became an apologist for American slavery and argued that blacks were naturally suited to slavery; Irish people, being a noble and honourable race, were not natural slaves. Building on this racist argument, he compared British domination over Ireland to Northern domination over the Southern states, and supported both Southern and Irish overthrow of their more powerful masters.[20] O'Brien's attitudes towards the South and slavery have strong echoes of Mitchel, and he explicitly compares the British-Irish conflict to the Northern-Southern one in the text; Mitchel's ideas that the Irish were unnaturally enslaved would have also complemented O'Brien's belief in his family's noble, heroic lineage. But O'Brien's attempts to engage with Mitchel in a personal way were, as he relates in the text, unsuccessful, as a letter seeking Mitchel's advice on Irish nationalist progress was rebuffed.

O'Brien's account of antebellum New Orleans testifies to its spirited public life and custom of public and private masked balls, military parades, and carnival – culminating in the tradition for which the city is now famous, Mardi Gras. O'Brien mentions parades led by the fire brigade held around the eighth of February, which he believed was George Washington's birthday. Washington's birthday was actually on 22 February and is usually now celebrated in the United States with a public holiday on the third Monday of February. Andrew Jackson's victory over the British in New Orleans on 8 January 1815 was also celebrated as a public holiday, so it is possible that O'Brien has remembered the wrong month. The most tempting theory is that O'Brien recalled an early public celebrations of Mardi Gras, a movable feast celebrated the day before the beginning of Lent, which can be between 8 February and 22 March. The first Mardi Gras crew, or organisational association, in the city of New Orleans was formed in 1857. However, New Orleans also held a military parade on Washington's birthday, led by the Continental Guards militia. In the absence of an army New Orleans organised its men into militias according to neighbourhood. Despite strong numbers on paper, these militia were severely underarmed and underattended. What they lacked in weaponry, however, each militia compensated for in dramatic, theatrical uniforms: for example, the Southern Rifles, a volunteer militia, 'dressed in green hunting shirts, buff leather knee britches buff top boots and black felt hats looped-up at the left with plumes.'[21]

In Chapter Five, O'Brien had the opportunity to defend the institution of slavery by supporting the Southern secession in the

American Civil War. Irish and German immigrants made up the largest immigrant groups in the war, but most of them fought for the Northern Union side, not the Southern Confederacy. Irish and Germans immigrants also composed 40 per cent of New Orleans's population at the end of the war, but were not generally seen as supportive of slavery, as they were sometimes competing against slaves in the labour market.[22] O'Brien enthusiastically enlisted as an assistant surgeon, on account of his medical training, but as in Nicaragua he did not take part in any fighting.

When New Orleans came under Union control in 1862 and the local economy collapsed, O'Brien exercised his foreign citizenship and negotiated his family's departure from the city. In Chapter Six, he returned to Ireland and settled in Cork, using the bookkeeping skills he had acquired in Louisiana to find employment. This relatively stable life permitted O'Brien to immerse himself in the growing Fenian movement. The 'Brotherhood' (later more formally known and referred to by O'Brien as the Irish Republican Brotherhood, or IRB) lacked organisation, funds and ammunition, though successfully recruited from within Ireland and the Irish communities in the United States and Britain. O'Brien had joined in New Orleans and smoothly resumed his involvement in Cork.

O'Brien is highly critical of Fenian organisation in Cork in the 1860s. He insists that, prior to the 1867 Rising, he had neither leadership nor influence, and that his warnings and advice regarding organisation and confidentiality fell on deaf ears.

In Chapter Seven, O'Brien found himself taking part in a revolution that lacked leadership, military strategy, supplies or discipline. Possessing some experience of marching and drilling, if not actually fighting, and later referred to as 'Colonel O'Brien', he assumed a leadership position when others declined to rise to the occasion. When a member of his group decided to attack a police barrack, he participated since he 'felt it unbecoming to me that another should be more daring than myself, so notwithstanding that I thought it imprudent'. He is anxious to portray himself as providing a moral compass to the troops under his command, ensuring justice for the poor, like the Robin Hood character Freney of the adventure literature he read as a boy; he rescues women and children, prevents his troops from firing on police officers, and ensures that a poor woman is paid for the bread his troops took. What O'Brien does not argue explicitly, as he might be expected to do, is that his actions were honourable even though he knew they were potentially suicidal. Rather than stressing that he knew the rising was doomed, but believed the symbolic gesture would be worth the effort, he makes great efforts to shield himself from blame and shifts the responsibility onto the original organisers and leaders (many of whom had been arrested in a series of sting operations in 1865 and 1866). The effect is that O'Brien presents himself as an accidental hero who rose to the occasion when he was let down by others, not as an opportunist who knew full well that the rising would be a failure. Lacking arms and ammunition, O'Brien's ad hoc army was forced to disperse, and he was soon arrested.

In Chapter Eight O'Brien is sentenced and imprisoned for his treasonous actions. Although it is now easy to see how disorganised the Fenian were, and how little threat they posed to public order, at the time they were viewed as a serious terrorist threat. English newspapers reported frequently, sometimes sensationally, about the movement and the arrests of members, which had been occurring regularly since the raid on the *Irish People* newspaper in 1865. The description of O'Brien's arrest in an English newspaper illustrates public fears about the extent of the Fenian menace and of Irish-American influence: 'Numerous arrests have been made here [Cork City]. A man named O'Brien, holding a high and lucrative position in this city, has been arrested for leading an assault on a police-station. He had been in America, and was known as an acquaintance of the head organiser, Stephens.'[23]

A Special Commission trial (outside the regular judicial session) was ordered by the government to investigate the risings and try the Fenian prisoners; this began in Dublin in April 1867 and in Cork a few weeks later. O'Brien had the rather dubious distinction of being the last person in the United Kingdom issued with a sentence to be executed by being hung, drawn and quartered. This brutal sentence, which would have involved public dismemberment of O'Brien's body, was already anachronistic in 1867, and had it been carried out in what was already a tense political environment it is likely that the public reaction would have been explosive. O'Brien argues that he never believed it would be carried out, and this is not just judgement in hindsight: by May the *Freeman's Journal* was suggesting that the judges and the government were looking for reasons to avoid capital punishment.[24]

Fenians prisoners awaited trial and began their sentences in locally-administered Mountjoy Prison in Dublin but then were sent to national prisons in England to serve their sentences: Millbank in London, which was for prisoners awaiting deportation to Australia, Portland in Dorset and Dartmoor in Devon.[25] O'Brien was sent to Millbank and then moved to Portland after he declined the opportunity to emigrate to Australia, citing family commitments. O'Brien's insistence that he was a devoted family man did not prevent him from taking part in a rising which, by his own accounts, he knew would be a failure – or explain his plan to evade capture by sailing to the United States. O'Brien's memoir does not even give the name of his first wife, though reading between the lines reveals many women aware of and supporting his and his comrades' political actions, including his mother who agreed to watch his children so that he could take part in the rising, and an unnamed teenage girl who ferried messages between Fenian leaders.

Prison conditions were harsh, as O'Brien relates, though his descriptions are more muted than many contemporary ones and his tone is stoical; this recalls Seán McConville's comment that the Fenian convict, as opposed to the ordinary prisoner, could be 'fortified by the correctness of his cause, and the moral reinforcement of his suffering'.[26] O'Brien was insistent, as Jeremiah O'Donovan Rossa had been before him, of his right to be treated as a political prisoner and not a common criminal. Perhaps anticipating an independent Ireland and fearful of creating communal discord, he is keen to emphasise that the warders in the Irish prisons were fair and professional, and that only the English prison officers were cruel.

In Chapter Nine, after a public campaign to amnesty Fenian prisoners and intervention from the new prime minister, William Ewart Gladstone, O'Brien emerged from prison in March 1869. If imprisonment was meant to discourage his treasonous tendencies or have a deterrent effect on would-be revolutionaries, it was a complete failure, for he immediately sought out members of the IRB for updates on the organisation's activities. Feted as a hero on his release, he also instantaneously saw the potential for electoral projects to advance Fenianism's goals. His new hero status gave him influence and associates, and he kept an open mind (or at least, he recalled that he had) about the new Irish Home Rule movement in Dublin.

O'Brien is strangely silent on Isaac Butt, the lawyer who had defended several of his fellow Fenians and was leading this new conglomeration. Butt's goal, in creating the new Home Government Association, was to bring together a diversity of influential Irish men to work towards a federalist, devolved government for Ireland within the United Kingdom. This initially attracted Irish Protestants and men with business interests. Some republicans were, as O'Brien recounts, opposed to the organisation, and others saw its potential but worried that by joining they would frighten conservative supporters.[27] The Home Government Association expanded, began successfully fielding electoral candidates in 1871, and an Irish Parliamentary Party soon took shape.

After some time to rest and recover from his prison ordeal (and a lengthy family holiday in France and Jersey, recounted in a Chapter Ten, which has been omitted), O'Brien stood as an Irish Parliamentary Party candidate in 1885. He won the Mayo South seat, which he held for ten years, then the Cork City seat in 1895, which he held until his death in 1905; not a gifted orator, he spoke little but was busied with treasury duties. O'Brien was first elected during one of the most exciting elections in Irish history, when the Irish nationalists won an unprecedented number of seats and agreed to give the Liberal Government their support in exchange for Home Rule legislation. Under the leadership of Parnell, the Party seemed poised to win an Irish parliament. This electoral success was partly predicated on a 'New Departure', negotiated in 1879, in which certain Fenians agreed to support Parnellite constitutional measures, which they had previously shunned as the antithesis of their physical force ideals.[28] The effect was that perhaps a quarter of the Parnellite Party had a Fenian past, including O'Brien.

Some Irish MPs embraced the Liberal alliance, joining the National Liberal Club and socialising with their English counterparts.[29] O'Brien describes his disapproval of such behaviour in his concluding chapter, a sombre reflection on the state of the Irish Parliamentary Party. Revelations about Parnell's personal life rocked the Party and led to nearly a decade of infighting and leadership contests, expressed in O'Brien's argument (contradicted by his own relationship with Webb and other colleagues), that the members of the Party were 'practically strangers' to each other. His old friend John O'Leary, who published his own memoirs in 1896, had rejected parliamentarianism and turned to new literary movements; he had also supported Parnell in the split, whereas O'Brien had quickly turned anti-Parnellite.[30] Through these events, it is possible to read O'Brien's entire memoir as a justification for his political choices and an affirmation of his righteousness, honour and patriotism, in the face of accusations that he had rejected his earlier Fenian ideals and become too close to the British establishment. This is the subdued conclusion to O'Brien's journey of 50 years dedicated to the liberty of Ireland, at home and abroad.

Chapter 1

[Early Years in Waterford]

Of the date of my birth I cannot speak with any pretence to accuracy. I have an indistinct recollection of having asked my mother a question on this subject when I was about twelve years old, and soon after I got from her an old savings-bank pass book – on a leaf of which my name was written and the date 2nd December 1831. But I have lately been told by my cousin James Vincent Cleary, now Archbishop of Kingston, Canada, that when he was parish priest of Dungarvan he had examined the register of births and that I was nearly two years older than I imagined – that there were but a few months between us. He did not give the date of my birth, nor say which of us is older.[1]

My father was Timothy O'Brien, my grandfather, Christopher O'Brien. He farmed about eighty acres of land at Duckspool, near Dungarvan. Of my father's brothers I remember the names of John, Jeremiah, James and Patrick. I think John was the eldest and Patrick the youngest. I do not remember that he had a sister. John and Jeremiah had gone to America before my birth, one of them, John I think, to Ohio, the other to New Brunswick or New Foundland.

The tombstone of my grandfather Christopher O'Brien was, I suppose still is, in front of the principal entrance to the church of Abbeyside. My elder brother Christopher told me that in the graveyard of Kilgobinet, a few miles from Dungarvan, on the slope of the mountain or hill which lies to the left of the road towards Kilmacthomas, he saw several tombstones belonging to the family.

My father's brother James (whose wife was the sister of a Father O'Brien) had one son named John. They went to Boston about 1853. The boy John was learning shoemaking.

William Smith O'Brien, whom I met in New Orleans about 1859, told me that a short time before his visit to America he had spent a day or so with my brother Christopher in Dungarvan.[2] He talked over the history of the O'Brien family with him and on his return home he had looked up documents and was satisfied that our family was descended from that branch of the Thomond O'Briens which settled in Waterford County in 1368.[3] My father died in 1853.

My mother, who died in Belfast in 1873 and whose remains I brought to Dungarvan, was daughter of Matthew O'Brien, a prosperous farmer who lived at Ballyguiry at the foot of Slieve Grine, three miles from Dungarvan on the left side of the valley leading to Cappoquin. He died at Aglish House, Aglish, then the residence of his only son James O'Brien. The age of my maternal grandfather was variously estimated at 108 to 112 years.

I remember being carried on the back of a man in my father's employment to an infant school kept by an old lady named Mrs Cassin. My next teacher was Mrs Dwyer. Her husband taught a senior boys' school in the same house. Many priests in Waterford diocese receive their early education – including a good amount of Latin and Greek – from him.

Punishments at Mrs Dwyer's were dispensed by her husband. I can call to mind Mr Dwyer laying me across his knees and whipping me. I think it was for having mitched from school.[4] I can remember having preferred the fields and green lanes to the school at that period of my life. But when I was in due time promoted to the senior school, possibly at the age of nine or thereabouts, I became ambitious to win a respectable place in my class. I was proud of my name and descent. I felt that I had in my veins the blood of an old, illustrious race and the desire to do nothing unbecoming such a descent was always strong in me.

In this way my love for Ireland gradually grew, till I felt as one *dedicated* to my country's service – till to live or die for Ireland was my one controlling desire.

When I was eight or nine years old Father Mathew, the great apostle of temperance, visited our town.[5] Without asking permission from anyone I took with me two sisters, who were younger than myself – went with them to the church where Father Mathew was then [page missing].

My recollections now begin to shape themselves more definitely. Though always shy and retiring in disposition I was during my boyhood a sort of leader and champion among my playmates.

My acquaintances with the literature of my times began with the life of Freeny the highway robber, whose adventures I first heard from the lips of the servants.[6] I later read the published account of his life. Freeny was hunted by English law. I don't know when I began to be against English law, but I was then against it and consequently I sympathised to some extent with Freeny, who set that law at defiance. As well as my memory services now, he was always kind to the poor. Sir William Harcourt, Chancellor of the Exchequer 1892–5, was not the first to levy taxes on a scale increasing as the wealth of the subject increased.[7] Honour to whom honour is due. Sir William most certainly was not the originator of that eminently just system for it was practiced by Freeny long before. Indeed I do not doubt that the system had been carried out by that bold outlaw Robin Hood and by his most distinguished predecessors.

It was, probably, soon after this that I had an opportunity of reading *The Battle of Ventry Harbour*. What intense delight this afforded me! It purports to describe an attempt made by Dara Down, the Monarch of the World, to invade and conquer Ireland. I can still picture to myself that great battle fought upon the sea shore, the terrible slaughter and how my heart swelled with the desire that I might be afforded an opportunity for emulating the prowess of the son of the King of Ireland, aged thirteen years, the bravest of the brave on that day so glorious for Ireland, for the Monarch of the World retired utterly defeated from the shores of Erin.[8]

Possibly I was not more than eight years old at the time I have just described, for I was no more than ten or eleven when my acquaintance with John O'Leary began, and I had then advanced beyond Freeny and Dara Down.[9] O'Leary's father was a merchant in Tipperary. Some of the members of the family frequently visited Dungarvan for sea bathing. Mrs Byrne, an aunt of John's, lived there and he and his sisters and brothers stopped with her when they came to Dungarvan. I think he attended at Mrs Dwyer's school for three or six months or more at this time.

Our families became intimate and I met John frequently. From the beginning I looked up to him and admired him. His intellectual capacity I recognised as considerably above mine. His high principles attracted me. They were higher than I had been accustomed to, in the matter of telling lies for instance. His influence upon me was decidedly good. His visits to Dungarvan were pretty regular during the summer months for some years. Then we drifted apart, but in 1848 I was proud to learn that he was imprisoned for being implicated in a plan to rescue William Smith O'Brien from Clonmel jail. My own feelings were well abreast with the most advanced politics, as I advanced in years. I deeply felt for the failure of Smith O'Brien's attempt at Ballingarry.[10] I was proud of him for the great sacrifices he had made. I felt that the people ought to have rallied to him and I believe they would have done so had they not been so utterly broken in spirit by the woeful famine.

The use of the Repeal Button comes back to my remembrance.[11] I remember Father Twomey, an Augustinian Friar, telling some of us youngsters how proudly he was wont to display it when he met neighbouring shoneen.[12]

Dungarvan boasted a band then and we were frequently treated to soul-stirring music. The enthusiasm of the crowds that followed the band was extraordinary. The inscription on the Repeal Button when O'Connell had been released from prison was 'Remember the 30th May 1844'. An effort was made to arouse the people to greater spirit which had received a set back upon his imprisonment. Previously the faith in O'Connell was almost so strong as our religious faith. We felt as if he could not fail, that if his moral force tactics should not succeed the popular belief was that he would then fall back on physical force which had greater attractions for the masses. I do not think we were able to perceive, as it was desired by O'Connell, that he was the victor in the encounter with the Government respecting the Clontarf meeting and in the law courts.[13]

Hitherto O'Connell had been unmatched as a lawyer, the invincible politician. He was in truth the uncrowned monarch of Ireland. But he had now been deprived of liberty illegally. It is true this was soon acknowledged to be illegal, but for this illegality no one suffered. His moral force position was no longer so strong and secure as it was believed to have been. If he had now fallen back on physical force, as the people certainly understood him to have intended, an indicator to this effect would at once have raised him higher than ever in the hearts of the people. Their hearts were sore when he did not hold his ground at Clontarf.

I suppose he never dreamt of falling back on physical force – that the speeches that set the blood on the people aflame were only an attempt to bluff the government and bring them to yield rather than face a rebellion. He was not, after his release from prison, any longer the mighty Tribune in whose hands the millions of the Irish people were as wax. The great Monster Meetings at Mallow, Tara and Mullaghmast – there was a growing discontent respecting the attempts of John O'Connell to pose as his father's alter ego and coming successor.

Popular feeling was running strongly in favour of men like Davis, Smith O'Brien and Duffy, and others being allowed to take prominent places in Conciliation Hall.[14] John O'Connell's conduct towards them was resented. It was hoped that his father would interpose and make matters right. And it was with consternation it was realised that he would not do this, but took the part of his son, who had flouted these men who by this time had won public regard.

The terrible Famine years were now upon us. The potato crop of 1844 had been abundant in quantity if indifferent in quality. Food was very cheap. Beef was as low as 3d per pound, potatoes 2d per stone, a hake weighing about eight pounds might have been had for 1 ½d or 2d.[15] I have seen heaps of small potatoes, possibly picked from those to be stored in pits, lying by the ditch as if left to rot. The month of February was the only summer-like month in 1845. There was no summer weather after that. I remember quite distinctly walking in the country a mile or more near Dungarvan in the month of July, having noticed an extra-ordinary stench as from rotting vegetable matter. It proceeded from some potato fields. A vapour hung over the country. I do not think there had been any talk of potato disease before. Each person was hoping that his own crop would escape, but before long it was found that the disaster was widespread. I record only what I saw with my own eyes, and therefore I speak not of the effects produced in other parts of the country.

The workhouses had been built in Ireland a few years before this, but they had been practically unused.[16] It was an insult to the poorest beggar to urge him or her to take shelter in the workhouse. But ere long the pangs of hunger – ruthless starvation – broke down the pride not only of the ordinary beggar but of countless thousands of labourers who had previously maintained their families by working for farmers and odd jobs, but largely by cultivating patches of potatoes, which were now all lost.

I have seen the workhouse – hitherto an object of contempt – besieged by thousands of starving creatures – a terrible encampment, each wretched family in a little group. No one was admitted without certain formalities, so that much time was consumed before they were admitted and many died while waiting for admission, but I believe a much greater number perished soon after they had entered – their poor bodies had been so completely famished and wasted they were unable to digest the yellow meal – which I believe the workhouse cooks did not then know how to prepare. The story was that the Indian corn meal was not half cooked, and in such a condition it was poison to those poor starved creatures and they perished in large numbers soon after admission to the workhouse.[17]

Almost every day starving men, women and children were seen on the footways of the town unable to move, lying, I might say, in the agonies of death. It was a terrible time! But how carefully the rights of property were guarded! Poor creatures found taking turnips or potatoes from a field were promptly sent to jail by a magistrate.

A few small farmers long held out. Those holdings from five to twenty acres soon had to give up the struggle and go to swell the ever-growing mass of pauperism. Of course whoever was able to do so left the country for America, chiefly. Many who could not meet such an expense were glad to go to England and Wales.

Dungarvan was in constant communication with the South Wales seaports and vessels: carrying over corn and chiefly oats and bringing back coal from Cardiff and Newport, culm from Swansea.[18] Thus South Wales afforded a refuge to many from our town and neighbourhood.

But while our poor people perished thus miserably, I say nothing of sufferings of the countless numbers who died in their own poor homes of famine and typhus fever. I did not see those fearful sights – they have been described by those who saw them – but I venture to say that what I saw then could not under similar circumstances have taken place in any country in the world in which anything pretending to be a responsible government existed – not even under the unspeakable Turk. It is almost incredible but it is absolutely true.

While our country was thus desolated, as many as twenty or more carts each laden with about a ton of wheat, oats, etc. would come from inland towns escorted by military and police. I have seen this many times. Occasionally a crowd of desperate men and women would make a dash upon the convoys, not without danger of course. Lives were lost, injuries were sustained and arrests were made. Not even the Sultan of Turkey would surely help to export the food of his people while famine raged among them. There was an abundance of food in Ireland – but it was of the best kind – the kind that would sell for money and would meet the rent of the landlords. A native government would have seen to the lives of the people first. The foreign government concerned itself about the landlords' rent. In my humble judgment a more hideous crime does not stain the pages of history!

Did the government really regret the famine? Its organ, *The Times*, rejoiced, gloated over the Famine, crying out, 'The Celts are gone with a vengeance!' Few nations have suffered as Ireland. What might have happened in 1848, if famine had not fallen upon the country, it is useless to speculate upon. The people were utterly broken and dispirited.

I think it was previous to 1847 that Richard Lalor Sheil MP accepted a Government appointment: Master of the Unit, or in charge of the British Embassy at Florence.[19] Sheil had been a follower of O'Connell – and as a Repealer had pledged himself not to accept any office or involvement under the Crown. His breach of the pledge aroused a strong feeling and his re-election was stoutly opposed. A Repeal Club then existed in the town. It included many of the younger businessmen and among them my elder brother Christopher. He was the Secretary of the Club. Several attempts were made to find a candidate to oppose Mr Sheil. One was John Augustus O'Neill of Bunowen Castle, another, Sir John Acton. Neither would consent. The belief among the members of the Club was that O'Connell induced them to decline.

My knowledge of these matters comes from my having copied for my brother the correspondence connected with the Election. Finally, when by four or five days remained to the date fixed for the election the men of the Club sent a deputation of four of the number, one of whom was my brother, to Cork to invite John Francis Maguire to contest the borough.[20]

Maguire came down. The fight was a stiff one. He lost by eight or eleven votes. It was not long till the borough was again vacant. Maguire contested again and was again defeated by eight or eleven votes. Ponsonby was opponent on this occasion.[21] After a long interval Dungarvan became vacant again. Maguire again came down and he was returned the third time.

It is unneccesary to say that the system of open voting prevailed at this time and all sorts of influences were employed against the Young Ireland Candidate.[22] Had the ballot then existed the popular candidate would have been triumphantly returned against Sheil.

I think it was in the autumn of 1848 that John O'Mahony was reported to have taken the field with 1,000 followers in the neighbourhood of Portlaw.[23] It was reported that he was moving towards Dungarvan. I believe many burned with anxiety to join him. I know I was very ready to do so. He did not come however, for his attempt was quickly suppressed. After this I felt terribly depressed – I was about 17 years old – and as there appeared to be no chance of a fight for Ireland I thought I would become a priest and I entered the diocesan seminary at Waterford as an ecclesiastical student.

I had not been long in Waterford College when rumours began to come in of an improved spirit among the people and of contemplated risings. I remember an essay being part of the work expected from the Humanity class to which I belonged, either at Easter time or previous to the summer vacation. I was so full of political feelings that my essay was a strong denunciation of the Saxon foe.

Before leaving College for the summer vacation or soon after my return home I had joined with all my heart the conspiracy set on foot by James Fintan Lalor of Tenakill, Queen's County.[24] During the vacation I went one day with the others – some if not all there were fellow students – to Carrick-on-Suir for the purpose of bringing back pike heads. We called at the house of one Hickey at Carrickbeg, where we were expected. We met Thomas Clark Luby.[25] He appeared to be quite a young swell to us country boys, as I might say. He was stretched on the grass outside the house and was reading a book on military tactics. He paid no attention to us. I next saw Luby at Portland Prison in 1868.

Hickey appeared to be a small farmer. A daughter of the family was sent to a blacksmith for our pikes and she brought back 100 pike heads – about twenty inches long including the shank to be fixed in the handle. The blades were diamond shape. Miss Hickey brought them in a covered handbasket.

The road from Dungarvan to Carrick was patrolled by mounted police, for the country was then, as it has been several times since, in a disturbed state. There was therefore some risk in bringing the pike-heads back with us.

This little affair came to a head at Cappoquin – as well as I remember, in the autumn of this year (1849). I heard nothing of the attack on the police barrack there until it had passed off – a poor fiasco. I suppose notice was not given me because I was so young.

It however came to the knowledge of the police authorities that I had something to do with the conspiracy. And I got warning that a warrant had been issued for my arrest. The Chief of Police was on friendly terms with my family. From a place of concealment I heard the police – who I suppose had come to arrest me – going through the premises. We owned two or three small vessels, about 100 tons burden or so – and one of them happened to be in the bay ready to sail for Cardiff. The boat was brought in for me and I went off to Cardiff. I visited several towns on the English Channel: Weymouth, Falmouth, Penryn, Truro, Plymouth, Portsmouth, etc.

I learned that Joe Brennan was at the Cappoquin affair. He was a writer – editor, perhaps – on one of the short-lived newspapers that took up John Mitchel's work when interrupted by his imprisonment, trial, conviction and deportation.[26] Brennan's paper was I think either *The Felon* or *The Tribune*. My first meeting with him was at New Orleans about 1857, to which I hope to refer later.

After I had spent less than two months in the south of England my people considered it safe that I should return to Ireland – but not to Dungarvan. My career as an ecclesiastical student was brief, for I had no idea of returning to the College. Indeed the President, Reverend Dr O'Brien, later bishop of Waterford, was anxious that I should return.[27]

At this time John Walton, my brother-in-law, was in business in Fermoy, buying oats and butter for shipment to England. I went to Fermoy and assisted him for about six months. Then my father took premises in Lismore putting me in charge, and there I bought oats which I sent to Dungarvan for shipments on board my father's vessels.

In Lismore I lived in a small house with only a man servant – who had been a soldier. He was a very handy man about house or horses. The following little incident will show how guileless I was. Nolan, my servant, had one morning failed to attend to his duties. I went to his room and found he was 'ill', he at all events said he was, and before paying any attention to my own wants I prepared and gave to him some breakfast. I would certainly have hesitated to do this had I known, what was apparently well known to the neighbours, that Mick's illness was due to drink. But of this I had not the least suspicion till shortly after.

From the autumn of 1849 to 1853 I assisted in my father's business at Fermoy, Lismore and Clonmel, buying oats and sending them to Dungarvan. He carried on with the assistance of my brother Christopher, who managed the business – extensive trade in importing timber, slates and coal, and exporting oats and butter.

My father died in 1853. And as I thought my brother assumed towards me too much of the style of the master to which I could not submit, after some consideration I decided to take up the study of medicine.

Chapter 2

Medicine Studies in Galway and Paris

I went to Galway in the autumn of 1854 about six weeks before the Matriculation Exam for the Queen's College began. With the exception of the eight or nine months at Waterford College 1848–9, my studies had terminated and I had left Mr Dwyer's school about 1845, 6 or 7. I remember that I was assisting in my father's business in 1847 and 1848. Consequently I was by no means fresh in the subjects required for the matriculation. However, I set to work with a will, and did so well with the help of a grinder that I not only matriculated easily but was encouraged to try for a scholarship, and I succeeded.[1]

I was a close student during my time at Galway. Every hour of the day was given to study of lectures except an hour or two for a solitary walk – a portion of which, in fine weather, was spent by the sea at Salthill listening to the melancholy music of the waves. Such was the regular and almost unfirm manner of my life in Galway. The only variation was that I visited at the homes of fellow students residing in the city perhaps half a dozen times.

The ordinary amusements and distractions of boys and young men had no attractions for me. I did not drink, smoke or take snuff or play cards. There was little during my ten or eleven months worth relating. Sometimes I attended that church of the Vincentians at the Claddagh. The scene from the gallery was striking – the red cloaks and red-brown petticoats of the women made contrasted beautifully with the light blue jackets and sailor-cut trousers of the men, each apparently capacious for a family.

Three other students lived in the house with me, and on the approach of St Patrick's day it was agreed that we should invite a number of friends to spend the evening at our rooms. I think twenty-one all told assembled.

We had an enjoyable evening – music, song and conversation – drink filling up intervals. But as the hours advanced, under the drink influence our guests became quarrelsome. I don't remember whether I had yet begun to use liquor, but I took it very sparingly, and it was very well for that night. For more than an hour – perhaps two hours – I had to make a round of the room sitting beside each in turn trying to check the angry words each was so anxious to hurl at his neighbour. I succeeded fairly well, but it was a great relief when it was time to separate.[2]

Father Peter Daly PP was then a great man in Galway. He was I think Chairman of the Harbour Board. I was in his Church one Saturday about to make my confession to him, when to my amazement he came out of the Confessional and soundly scolded a man who was making his confession – possibly he had not begun, possibly he had concluded, or he might have gone to the Confessional for some other purpose than to confess, which indeed is most likely.[3] Certainly if he proposed to himself to take Father Peter at a disadvantage by presenting himself at the Confessional he did not gain much from it. For he left the Church – without an inch of a tail. What the row was about I had no idea. Fr Peter spoke with so much vehemence his words were, to me, indistinguishable.

I don't think I troubled Father Peter that day, I rather think I sought another priest. From another incident which I observed poor Father Peter must have been naturally irascible. He was preaching one Sunday in 'Father Daly's chapel' adjoining the Convent of the Sisters of Mercy. The church was flagged and when he began to preach the people rose from their knees and gathered towards the altar – the better to hear him. While he was speaking a little child, about two years old, came in from the street and toddled across the space left vacant by the crowding towards the altar, every time footfall sounding distinctly. Father Peter was greatly annoyed and cried out in angry tones: 'Take that dirty little thing out of that.' The little child was quite cleanly got up I must say.

Some of my fellow students were boys apparently not more than fifteen or sixteen years old, whose homes were distant and who lived in rooms as independently as if they were fully grown young men. I thought then and I think now that it was very rash of the parents who had exposed those boys to such a life.

On Saturdays those students who were studying Botany usually went on an excursion with the Professor Melville. Beyond attending his lectures which were generally interesting I knew nothing of Professor Melville. He was generally liked – was rather a universal favourite. He was a Scotchman – his sympathies were not pro-Irish, but rather the other way.[4]

One Saturday about twenty-five of us went by boat, the ordinary fishing boat, about fifteen tons. One of the party brought a concertina on which he was a good performer. We had many nationalist Irish airs and songs. I suppose three-fourths of us were ardent nationalists. Somehow I was recognised at their leader. I dare say that I was in conversation pretty outspoken when politics were on the topic – though I do not recollect anything of a political character during my time at the College but the incident I am referring to.

There were some half-a-dozen students in the boat whose opinions were anti-national. The presence of Dr Melville encouraged them to an amount of self-assertion which they would not otherwise attempt – and, after we had a number of our favourite tunes they called for 'Boyne Water,' 'Croppies Lie Down,' or some such anti-national tunes. The concertina performer was I think inclined to accede, then hesitated, and looked to me for guidance. I objected. There was something approaching to a row in the boat, but it was quickly avoided – the numerical superiority of the nationalists was so obvious.

There was no more music. Professor Melville was very angry, but no one cared. The Nationalists were proud of having declared themselves openly. Melville had his revenge for he gave no prize for Botany that year. I thought I ought have got it.

I spent about nine months in Galway and when the summer vacation began I went to Dungarvan. It must have been about this time, after my return home, that the following remarkable incident occurred. One evening taking a walk with one of my sisters, about nine or ten p.m. (it was mid-summer), we had not yet left the outskirts of the town and there was a long row of small houses – mere cabins – on our right. We were going in a northwest direction. Suddenly I observed a bright yellow light leaving the sky on our left at an elevation of about 35°. It shot down slowly to the place in which my sister and I were. It appeared to strike the ground some few hundred yards to our left, it gradually advanced towards us – we were still walking – my sister's hand on my arm. The light continued to advance and it crossed the road in such a manner that it formed a broad band of yellow light in the middle of which we found ourselves. It then advanced up the side of the cabin on our right. The light slowly withdrew as it came and reentered the sky apparently at the point from whence it issued. The belt of yellow light it formed on the road was about six or eight feet. My sister trembled and was frightened when she found herself in the bright light. I was not in the least disturbed by it. I was of course astonished. I do not think my sister perceived it until she was in the middle of it. I have never seen, heard or read of anything like it.[5]

I returned to Dungarvan from Galway for the summer vacation. Whether I met John O'Leary then and learned in person of his intention to go to the Paris in October, accompanied by his brother Arthur, or whether I learned this from correspondence, I do not recollect. Arthur was to study Art, John to read anything and everything in aimless fashion.

O'Leary was a great attraction for me notwithstanding that I very strongly condemned some of his doings. For instance an impudent letter which he wrote to the newspapers on the subject of the Queen's Colleges – then denounced by the Catholic hierarchy. The latter was I think addressed to the archbishop of Cashel. He said in the letter that, the condemnation of the Irish bishops notwithstanding, he was determined to avail of them (the Queen's Colleges), or word to this effect. I do not think that the term poppycock is too strong to apply to such language, especially when addressed by a very young man to the dignitaries of the Catholic Church – to which he belonged. But indeed his position in regard to the Church has not been very clear since that time (about 1851 to 1853). His faith had in some way become unsettled. But though he could not at this time or at any subsequent time as far as I know be called a Catholic, I do not think he had adopted any other faith. To me it has always appeared that his loss of faith was due to pride of intellect. I regretted it very much.[6]

I decided to go to Paris and to carry on my medicine studies there. I set off about the beginning of October or end of September 1855. The First Paris Exhibition was then open. I remember having there seen Hogan's study of Brian Boru as a boy.[7]

I took a room in an old house in the Rue Lacépède for which I paid thirty francs a month.[8]

My resources were very limited and I economised rigidly. I attended lectures at the École de Médecine as well as clinical lectures at various hospitals – La Pitié, La Charité, Hôtel Dieu. I read and dissected diligently.

I was soon able to understand the lectures, but I am bound to say my going to Paris was a mistake, as far as the study of medicine was concerned. The winter was much more severe than I had ever before experienced, yet the air was so dry I did not much feel the low temperature. I wore no overcoat, and in my room, brick-tiled – it was an old house – I rarely had fire. With a rug wrapped about my feet and legs I was able to read quite comfortably.

The lecture room – amphitheatre – of the École de Médecine presented the most curious collection of students I have ever seen – every age, from 16 to 70. Every condition, from the perfumed and bejewelled dandy to the man who had evidently slept in his greasy looking *capote* and whose boots had never seen blacking since they had left the shop.[9] The lectures were always listened to with attention.

It was interesting to observe the rapidity with which a notice concerning any matter interesting to the students circulated in the amphitheatre and without the slightest noise. The notice, written on two pieces of paper each marked '*Faites passer*' was generally set in motion from the middle bench – one passed from hand to hand down – the other in like manner, up to the top in a very few minutes, each student reading it and passing it on.[10]

When I started for Paris I had a certain grammatical knowledge of French but I soon found that one may read French readily but be able to understand very few words of the spoken language. After a short time however my ear gradually became accustomed to the sound. My great difficulty was the want of a sufficiently extensive vocabulary. And in help with this difficulty I carried a pocket dictionary which I constantly produced when short of a word.

There was a restaurant near the École de Médecine, at which I frequently dined after the 4 o'clock lecture. It was then crowded with students. For the slender purses an appetising dinner was obtainable for 24 *sous*: soup, 2 *plats* of meat, bread, vegetables and what I think went by the name of *vol au vents*: young mushrooms with flavory [*sic*] sauce, presented as a small pie. A *carafon* (1/8 of bottle) of *vin ordinaire* was also included.

It was amazing to observe the waiters at that restaurant. One of them would take orders from I think not less than ten or more at a time. The waiter would return with the *plats* piled high and lay before each person what he had ordered. The orders were taken verbally only – yet a large number of them were rapidly executed with extraordinary accuracy.

I had been a few weeks in Paris when John O'Leary and his younger brother Arthur came over. They appear to have met en route James Whistler – the distinguished painter and etcher of those days.[11] He came with them to the Hotel Corneille, Rue Corneille, Whistler bringing with him from London a set of utensils for cooking. It was in O'Leary's room he produced them the first day I saw them. In something like a tripod a lamp was suspended – over this was hung a deep tin pan. He cooked an omelette on that occasion.

Whistler was queer looking chap – about 5ft. 3in., pale, sallow face, features no way striking or pleasing. An abundance of black, curly hair, slight moustache, eyes dark, sparkling, impudent looking; perky, cock sparrow style, he constantly sang the 'Ratcatcher's daughter'. He wore a low crowned black felt hat on the side of his head.

Scarcely a day passed of which I did not spend a portion with John O'Leary and his brother. I frequently met Whistler in their rooms. I remember a day he sketched O'Leary's head in my note book, it was in Rembrandt style. I regret that I have lost that notebook.

It was in the autumn of 1855 that James Whistler began his studies in Paris. In the same street in which I lived John Martin and Kevin Izod O'Doherty with his wife Eva (née O'Kelly) who had been frequent and highly appreciated contributors to the columns of *The Nation* newspaper, when it was in its prime. She was best known as 'Eva of the *Nation*'.[12] All three lived in the same pension in the Rue Lacépède.

It was a great pleasure to me to go to their rooms with the two O'Leary's to visit them. Eva was always amiable and kind – she took a fair share in the conversation – her ability was decidedly superior to her husband's. She was a little above middle height, with wavy, glossy black hair, complexion dark, face rather large and square. Her features I cannot recall to mind but her expression was always pleasing, agreeable and placid. Kevin O'Doherty was about 5ft 10in. in height – and at the time I speak of about 32 years old. He was a fine young man with hair rather darker than brown.

In 1848 on the suppression of John Mitchel's newspaper he had started another paper to continue the same propaganda. One of them was *The Tribune*, the other was *The Felon*. I do not recollect which of them was O'Doherty's – he appears to have acted a manly part in connection with the newspaper, was tried for treason felony and sentenced to a term of transportation to Van Dieman's Land.

A short time before 1855 he had been released, married Eva, to whom he had long been engaged. He settled in Paris to renew and complete his medical studies. Later on he emigrated to Queen's Land, Australia, in the chief town of which, Brisbane, he became a successful practitioner. I think it was at the General Election of 1886 he joined the Irish Parliamentary Party, having been elected for [——]. He did not remain long in Parliament.[13]

John Martin has filled so conspicuous a place in Irish politics from 1848 down to his death in 1875 it can hardly be necessary for me to say anything of him. But should these 'Reminiscences' be ever given to the public they may fall into the hands of persons who may not have had opportunities of learning what manner of man was John Martin.

For years I had observed his letters to the Irish nationalist newspapers. At one time his address was Kilbroney, Loughshore, County

Down. His language whether written or oral had always the true ring. He appeared to see the truth of Irish political questions, almost unerringly. No matter how mild his words there was no mistaking their meaning. A more amiable, kindly, gentle, charitable man I never met. His charity towards the guilty was in my opinion extravagant, almost culpable at times. He was never without a kind word for anyone whose conduct would be the subject of discussion – no matter though all others were unanimous as to the man's villainy.

Martin was about 40 years of age when I first met him at the Rue Lacépède. He was deformed owing to fall when he was a baby in arms. His nurse concealed the injury until it was too late to apply remedies, and the sad consequence was that he was deformed for life.

His face was angular – prominent cheek bones, nose well shaped, fairly large, straight, chin well developed, and mouth very pleasing – always wearing a welcoming smile for his friends. His hair, beard and moustache were fair.

I like Martin very much. He was a good Christian man and a self-sacrificing patriot. He was a life-long friend of John Mitchel though in character they were so unlike. He married a sister of John Mitchel some ten years later than the time of I write of; she survived him and is I think living now (1895).

The conversations during those visits to O'Doherty's room in Rue Lacépède were a great pleasure to me. The company was nearly always the same: Mr and Mrs O'Doherty, Martin, John and Arthur O'Leary, and myself. Occasionally J. P. Leonard would come – and on a very few occasions an uncle of O'Doherty who was I should say then about seventy years old. This gentleman had in earlier years made a fortune in Canada and had come to France to enjoy it. But in some way he lost everything, in some way which I do not now remember. He returned to Canada to repair his shattered finances, made another fortune though of more moderate extent, and on its proceeds he was living comfortably. When he returned to Paris he used to be accompanied by an elderly female, called his *Bonne*, who waited for him and took charge of him returning home.[14]

Dominoes was a frequent game during those evening visits. We sometimes had other games which I forget. We always had tea prepared by Eva. Before leaving we generally retired to Martin's room for a smoke. I had by this time taken to the pipe, having been mistakenly assured that it was necessary for the dissecting room, but I found this to be a mistake. Martin became a heavy smoker during transportation or on account of the asthma from which he suffered. He had nearly twenty pipes in his own room, and as far as I observed he filled each every single night and smoked them all. His pipe stems were nearly three feet long.

Of J. P. Leonard I have not much to say though for many years there was no Irishman living in Paris so well known. He did not appear very often during our visits to O'Doherty's room, and I was at his residence not more than twice I think.

I heard him say he was brought from Cork to Bordeaux at the age of eight – and he lived in France, chiefly in Paris, for the rest of his life. In 1848 he took his place at the Barricades. For his service he received a small pension and was granted letters of naturalisation free of charge. They would have cost about £40. Those who had known him for years were surprised when they heard of his being naturalised for they had always supposed him to be a Frenchman.

Leonard was always prominent in any movement concerning Ireland when it was possible to arouse sympathy in France and he was always respected by the chief men of Irish descent in France, such as Marshall McMahon, Viscount O'Neill de Tyrone, etc.

My sojourn in Paris effaced from my mind an old, fond delusion! I was full of the idea of the great services Irishmen had rendered to France for many years since the Siege of Limerick. The various Irish brigades, the half a million Irishmen at the cost of whose lives France won glory on many a hard-fought field of battle. In my youth the idea strongly prevailed among young Irishmen that the memories of the Irish brigades were still alive in the hearts of Frenchmen – strong enough to prove a powerful bond of brotherhood between the two peoples. I should not be surprised if even to this day some remains of these old feeling still survive in the hearts of Irishmen. I do not think Frenchmen reciprocated these feelings in 1855. The existence of these feelings in the hearts of Frenchmen in the year of Grace 1895 is I think still more improbable.

In 1855 the name of France would have worked enthusiasm in an Irish crowd in almost any part of Ireland. But in that year the name of Ireland would be practically unknown and unnoticed in a French crowd in almost any part of France. There is a good philosophical explanation for this – but it does not satisfy me – I am not philosopher enough for that. I do not think sympathy for France is now as vivid as it was in 1855 amongst Irishmen – the old memories grow less distinct with the lapse of time when there is nothing to recall them. On the other hand, the anti-Catholic spirit which has animated French governments since the establishment of the Republic in 1870 has caused great pain to Catholic Ireland. The religious feeling in Ireland is as strong as the political, and in no country in the world is either stronger. There is no sacrifice the Irish people would hesitate to make for religion or country.

I think I am in these respects a typical Irishman – in defence of the rights of the Catholic Church, as in the defence or assertion of the rights of my country there is no sacrifice of goods, liberty or life I would hesitate to make. Would it be possible to rekindle a love of France in the hearts of our people? Most certainly! How? Let France make it known that if the people of Ireland still desire the independence of their country and are willing to fight for it that she will help them. A danger for England? Yes – a danger which England has herself to thank for.

Gladstone by his Home Rule proposals planned a road by which Ireland might enter into the political system of the United Kingdom and become a de facto and a content integral member thereof. But the Tory-Unionist party, being in Irish affairs the tool of the Irish landlords, would have none of this. They may see the desirability of conciliating Ireland in the interests of the Empire. But the Irish landlord is on the back of the British Tory.

I could conceive Ireland happy, contented and prosperous under Gladstone's Home Rule measure and jogging along harmoniously as a member of the United Kingdom. I do not think it possible for Ireland to abandon her aspiration and her struggle for autonomy and I sincerely trust she will pesist until her efforts are crowned with success.

Contrasting my early impressions of London and Paris – London was gloomy, dark, depressing. Paris on the contrary was bright, dazzling, exhilarating. I returned home to Dungarvan in bad health – I suppose about the end of May or beginning of June 1856. The effect upon my health of less than twenty months close study and meagre diet had been very severe. On the morning of the Matriculation Exam at the Queen's College Galway I – who had a few months before been muscular, strong and active – in perfect health, fainted three times in my room before going to the Examination Hall.

After having been confined to bed for several weeks I went to Dublin to consult Sir Dominick Corrigan the most distinguished M. D. in Dublin at the time.[15] He visited me several times in my lodgings, and later for some weeks after I called on him many times. He was most kind and attentive, but for all my visits he would accept only the nominal fee of £2, because I was a medical student.

When I was convalescent Corrigan advised me to give up study and 'knock about' for a while – an advice which I followed pretty thoroughly.

Chapter 3

[With William Walker in Nicaragua]

_____

When I made up my mind to take Sir Dominic Corrigan's advice, the plan I had out for myself was to endeavour to gain some military experience which might prove of use in Ireland's cause. I decided to join Walker in Nicaragua. Doubtless love of adventure had also something to say to my taking such a cause. I am certain neither motive would have been of sufficient force had not also Walker's schemes been presented to me in such a light as to be beneficial to humanity at large.[1]

Walker was an adventurer, described as personally pure, temperate, honest, and fearlessly brave, who appeared to have been 'led away by an unquestioning belief in his destiny.' At the time I speak of he had [illegible] to be elected President of Nicaragua, a Central American republic, and his government had been acknowledged by the United States. An expedition in his support was being organised at New Orleans.[2]

Before leaving Dungarvan I procured a simple outfit such as I thought would suit: a blue woolen shirt with turndown collar, worn with a belt outside the pants, a black silk neckerchief and felt hat.

At this time strange scenes were being enacted in that part of Central America called Nicaragua. The gold discoveries in California a few years earlier had attracted great crowds to the gold fields. Large numbers of these were of course failures and as a result these failures were ready for anything that might turn up.

The normal state of things then (and I believe to this day) in several of the Central American republics, in matters relating to the Presidency was: no sooner than a President had been elected that immediately a cabal was formed against him. León was I think the name of the President who ruled in Nicaragua at the time I write of.[3] When he was elected a few years earlier, the usual cabal was formed against him. And finding himself in great straits he conceived the idea of inviting a band of those ex-gold diggers from California. They comprised specimens of probably every race of white men on the earth – but in Nicaragua they were known as Americanos.

The Americanos enabled León to make head against his enemies. And in gratitude or possibly constrained there to his allies and supporters were made citizens of Nicaragua. He could scarcely have anticipated what was soon to follow from this.

When Leon's term of office expired a new election for President came on, and General William Walker, the leader of the Americanos, was elected. Whether this was a fair and honest election I have never heard – but what I heard in New Orleans somewhat later, viz: at one election the Irishmen practice great terrorism at the polling booths. While on another occasion the last election which had taken place before I landed there (February 1, 1857) the Native Americans disguised as Red Indians went on horse-back through those districts which were inhabited by Irish and Germans and shot down with revolvers numbers of people in the streets and at their doors.[4] This was for the purpose of striking terror in view of the approaching election.

When such things could have taken place in the important city of New Orleans what might not one suppose to have been possible about the same time. It is however quite possible that Walker's election was a well within the lines of legality as elections were ordinarily carried out in Nicaragua then – or perhaps even at the present (1895).

Walker was at all events elected and of course a cabal was formed against him. I think he maintained his position for one term (two years?) and was elected for a second term. I am not quite clear about this, but such is my impression. Walker's base of operations was in the United States. He was financed, as I had reason to think later on, by some wealthy firms – among them Garrison of New York.[5]

In the latter part of November 1856 I left Liverpool in the sailing ship 'Kossuth' bound for New Orleans.[6] The voyage which occupied seventy days was most dull and uneventful. The weather immediately preceding the sailing had been very stormy and we had among our passengers parties who had, within the previous week, been shipwrecked in the Mersey or a short distance from the mouth of the river. Some had been twice shipwrecked.

The first night after leaving Liverpool our ship was for a short time in danger near Holyhead. She took the ground lightly. In working down channel the wind drove her closer to the shore than was desirable. It was very dirty weather and it was with difficulty a light on shore was made out. Fortunately the tide was rising, and in the course of an hour or so the ship was got out of her difficulty. It if had been an ebb tide I believe that voyage might have ended there.

I may say that was the only mishap of our voyage – except that after we had been a few weeks at sea a storm came upon us one night. It made a tremendous hubbub among the steerage passengers. The lashings of their luggage broke loose and certainly the [illegible] made sufficient noise. During that storm a young man, steerage passenger, had his collar bone broken. And as there was no doctor on board, the number of passengers being less than that which makes it obligatory, I attended to the young man.

I think we must have had something like fifty Germans among the passengers. And it was very entertaining when in the afternoons about twenty of the males assembled amid ship to sing. They had evidently been trained at school. It was very pleasant, a most pleasing interruption to the general monotony of the voyage.

The clouds of course were a constant cause for wonder and admiration – the wonderful presentations of piled up mountains, immense collections of beasts and birds, etc. It is extraordinary what in the course of seventy days of such a voyage what foolish things one feels ready to attempt. In conversation one day a challenge was thrown out among the half-dozen passengers who occupied the cabin. It came from one of ourselves, viz: to climb up the main mast and place a hand on the cap – the top of the mast. There were of course the usual ladders as far as the two first sections of the mast but none to the third section of it – only ropes. I took up the challenge and in a few minutes had my hand on the cap and returned to the deck without mishap.

The weather was exceedingly calm at the time – there were no waves – but the ship occasionally shook and swerved from the action of the ground swell, as I believe it is called, and to a landsman a lurch of that kind was a serious matter holding on by a single rope by the topmast of a 2,000-ton ship. There was therefore more danger in the attempt than I knew of.

When we were off the island of Cuba I was one of a few who ventured to take a swim, jumping from the ship's boat. I have felt the water so strong and so buoyant – it was as if you could not sink in it. This also was not without danger since it was a place known to be frequented by sharks.

By this time everything bearing the name of tobacco had vanished in smoke and it was with great pleasure we came across a small trading vessel which had left Cuba the day before. We got a good quality of fine cigars and tobacco, honey, fruits and vegetables from this vessel.

The weather during our voyage had been very fine and, after the first few days, warm throughout. I do not think that, after we had got south of the Bay of Biscay, we encountered more than six or eight days of stormy weather during the whole voyage. This was now coming to a close.

It must have been the 29th or 30th January 1857 when we arrived at the mouth of the great river, the Mississippi – which, tracing it back to the beginning of its mighty tributary the Missouri, has its source more than 3,000 miles away in the Rocky Mountains.

The previous two months we enjoyed a tropical summer heat, but at the mouth of the Mississippi the air in the morning before it had been warmed by the sun was cold, raw and damp. It felt very uncomfortable after the warm weather we had been experiencing. I think this condition of the atmosphere was largely if not entirely due to the ice and frozen snow carried down by the river from the far away mountains. The immense volume of water poured out into the Gulf of Mexico by the Mississippi must affect the waters of the Gulf. That the temperature of the river was much below that of the sea at the time I know – for I drank more than once of the river water while going up to New Orleans. Unless my memory is at fault I would say I observed pieces of ice in the river water.

It is something to notice with wonder the extent to which the Gulf of Mexico is being filled up by the soil washed from the Rocky Mountains and deposited in the Gulf after having been carried down so many thousands of miles by the Missouri and the Mississippi. The river water which we drank while descending the river was the water of the river. It was of course taken from the surface of the river – from which, naturally, the soil carried down had to some extent been precipitated. As compared with the water in the depths of the river, what we got was comparatively clear of earth or soil. Yet, letting a glass of this water stand for a quarter of an hour, you would find nearly one fourth of it as mud as the bottom of the glass.

I do not remember whether we delayed more than one day at the mouth before ascending the river. While waiting, the Captain brought with him a few, of whom I was one, when he called on an official of some kind who lived at the mouth of the river. The domestics of this house were negroes, as black as coal, and I think had never seen a negro before. And when the woman brought us refreshments it was with considerable repugnance I received anything from her hands.

Two powerful tugboats – gripping at each side – carried the ship through the Bar, our keel ploughing through it to the depth of eighteen to twenty-four inches. Our ship's draught was, I think, 19 feet. Having crossed the Bar one tug sufficed. Indeed I think our tug had two ships. Some tugs had four smaller vessels. Our ship was moored to the levée about eight a.m. on the first of February.

An hour or two later the Captain took me and another young man passenger ashore and made a call upon some people he was acquainted with. This was my first introduction to a rocking chair of which there were more than one in the room. I took the chair tentatively and rather timorously as something that possible play me a trick [*sic*], and I landed safely into its arms. My companion on the other hand approached his chair in bold, manly fashion, and he quickly had his reward, for placing himself on the edge of the seat, the chair slid back and tumbled over him.

This was but a passing through visit of mine to New Orleans. It afterwards became my home for many years. I shall therefore bring in description of the city and its approaches after my return from Nicaragua.

I have already referred to Joseph Brennan as having edited one of the journals that took the place of John Mitchel's *United Irishman*. He had been engaged in the events at Cappoquin in which Fintan Lalor's conspiracy ended. I now found him a leading journalist in New Orleans – a recognised political power. I think I called on Joe Brennan the day I landed.

New Orleans seldom escapes a visitation from Yellow Fever for more than two or three years.[7] And during such a visitation some few years before 1857 Brennan was attacked by the fever. It was said that his doctor dosed him so heavily with quinine that while he recovered from the fever he became quite blind from the excessive use of quinine. During his blindness he wrote a very fine piece of poetry portraying his own feelings under the sad circumstances. When I met him he had recovered sight but only very imperfectly.

He was married to a sister of John Savage another well-known Irishman in those days. I think he was also a '48 man.[8] I asked Brennan to recommend a place where I might live at moderate expense and he gave me a letter of introduction to a Mrs Connolly who kept a boarding house on Julia St in the 1st district. Brennan told me that D'Alton Williams, another well-known '48 man, was married to a daughter of Mrs Connolly.[9]

I did not long delay acquainting Brennan with my desire of joining General Walker in Nicaragua. He told me though he could procure me the necessary facilities. And with that object he soon introduced me to Pierre Soulé.[10] He must be the same man of whom I have a hazy recollection, as having 15 or 20 years earlier, made a noise in the world through a quarrel with a M. Turgot at Madrid,[11] one or both of these gentlemen being attached to the French Embassy at Madrid. I think the quarrel was due to an offense offered to the wife of one of them (Soulé's wife, I think). A duel followed in which if I am not mistaken Turgot suffered and Soulé had to resign his post.

Soulé gave me an appointment on Walker's staff and very soon I was on board a steamer bound for San Juan or Greytown, a seaport of Nicaragua on the Mexican Gulf. The voyage to San Juan has left little impression on my mind beyond this trifling incident. While sitting in the steamer's saloon a game of cards was in progress. It was either

Euchre or Poker – American games, the names of which I had heard in New Orleans but had never played. After a time one of the four players retired from the game. Thereupon the other three invited me to join and keep the game alive. I told them that I did not know the game. They however pressured, and said it was easily learned and they would teach me. I consented, on their promising they would not be annoyed with my bad play. Strange to say, I won steadily until I observed that the others were displeased and appeared to think that my ignorance of the game was only pretended. When I noticed this I quickly lost what I had won and retired from the game.

The harbour of San Juan (pronounced – San Wan) has rather a narrow entrance. It is almost landlocked by a sandy strip called Punta Arenas (Sandy Point) which stretches in front of the harbour leaving a narrow entrance on the extreme right. I think Punta Arenas joins the land on its extreme left.

I do not remember whether we made any delay here. The small river steamer we expected to take us up the river San Juan (which discharges its waters into the Bay of San Juan) came down the river soon after our arrival. Our voyage up the river was slow and tedious, so much so that I think I may put in here rather a strange experience. During the three or four weeks I has spent in New Orleans I had become sleepless to an alarming extent – how to account for it I do not know. But for the fortnight before I left for Nicaragua I had scarcely slept at all. I became desperate, and I bought an ounce of Laudanum and I took half of it in one dose.[12] It however acted on me rather as a stimulant when I hoped it to produce sleep. I took the other half, with the same result.

The same evening I was taken by a gentleman I met in the Boarding House to the house of a friend where he was to spend the evening. While there, I drank three tumblers of punch, which I had never attempted before and very rarely since. I also danced a good deal. The consequence was I had a splendid and refreshing sleep that night.

And now – on the little steamer ascending the San Juan. The accommodation is of the scantiest kind – my sleeping place was on a deck, a framework of strong [illegible] – and upon this I slept comfortably, wrapped in a blanket with my bag for a pillow in the open air.

We were several days on this steamer and sometimes we bivouacked on shore. On one occasion while on land we were visited by a very heavy soaking rain, against which we were but ill protected. My tent was a blanket, two corners of which were tied to branches of trees, the other corners being fastened to the ground. The blanket, thus secured, sloped like one side of a roof. This was my only protection against sun or rain and under this I slept with a blanket over me. The heavy downpour of rain came during the night and of course I was thoroughly soaked. With morning happily came a warm sun.

I had with me a large overcoat which happily for this occasion had long loose sleeves. I divested myself of everything I had on me, and my coat, having been somehow protected from the rain, was quite dry. I inserted my legs into the sleeves, and so made myself quite comfortable, though scarcely presentably for parade, while my clothing dried in the sun.

When I had made up my mind to visit Nicaragua, I had that coat specially made by a Dungarvan tailor under my direction. I do not pretend to say that I contemplated wearing it in the manner above described, when I had the sleeves made so wide. That was perhaps an exaggeration of the fashion of the period. Certainly, the fashion served me a good turn on the occasion. The manner in which I utilised this coat would have done credit to Robinson Crusoe. Indeed, not one of the illustrations in that delightful book shows Robinson in stranger garb than mine on that day. Fortunately I had no visitors nor had I any occasion to present myself before anyone – even for my rations. I rather suspect that the whole party, some 200, were little better prepared for inspection than I at that time myself.

How we spent the weeks then I am now unable to recall. All the incidents I can recollect might fit into one week – yet there are six weeks to be accounted for. I had not been long with this crowd when the abominably vile language generally indulged in so disgusted me I could not endure remaining within ear shot – so I pitched my little tent at a distance from the main body. I am happy to say I have, from my boyhood, been always sensitive respecting bad language. I took such dislike to the ordinary conversation among young men that as I grew up I would have none of their company, their conversations being generally course and I had not a single companion in my native town. My company consisted of my sisters – two younger and one older than myself.

When I cannot avoid listening to blasphemous language an ejaculation comes to my lips: 'Blessed be God', 'Blessed be the name of Jesus', or some other according to the nature of the bad language. Amongst Americans I found blasphemy more common and more daring than I had ever heard before. But nothing that I had previously experienced at all prepared me for the fearful language of the men with whom I now found myself associated.

The hardships, such as they were – meagre fare and camping on the ground, cutting our way through dense vegetation of brushwood and brambles, getting wet with dew at night and being dried by the sun in the morning – these did not trouble me in the least, though I had only a short time previously recovered from a severe illness which left me greatly reduced in physique. But the blasphemous and obscene language of those troubled and pained me very much.

We were one day encamped at the junction of the San Juan and Serapiqué rivers; we must have passed several days there. The Serapiqué divided Nicaragua from Costa Rica. This place had evidently been an old camping ground – for there were stakes driven down by the margin of the river and fastened to those were several large empty boxes, in which rifles had been packed. Holes were bored at the end of the boxes and as they floated in the river they were partly filled with water.

The river bank was muddy and unfit for bathing. We had had a rough march – temperature between 80° and 90° with atmosphere rather humid.[13] The march, under such conditions, left me in a condition to appreciate a dip in the river. Consequently I did not delay undressing and taking possession of one of the aforementioned rifle boxes. I reclined therein, as well as the dimensions permitted. I think it was about five feet long or thereabouts, and for an hour or more I enjoyed quite a luxurious bath, the water coming in freely. I was in fact suspended in the water of the river.

Here I may give a specimen of the rations. Our rations were:

Biscuits: as good as could be desired, and for me at least, in quantity abundant.

Salt pork: quantity sufficient, the quality I think was only indifferent.

Coffee: the green berry, dried of course, the quantity sufficient to make a pint prepared for drinking.

The pork was roasted for me by a companion to whom I gave half for his trouble.

The coffee I first roasted in my tin rammiken [*sic*]. I then crushed the berries in the same rammiken, with the butt end of a bayonet, after which I took the same rammiken to the river, allowed the water to nearly fill it. Then putting it on the fire I boiled it. Not often have I relished a cup of coffee so thoroughly as I then did what I had thus myself so roughly prepared.

We must have spent a month on our very slow progress up the river San Juan. I believe this slowness was due to the difficulty of communicating with General Walker – who was on the Eastern or Pacific side of the country.

From leaving the town of San Juan until we returned to it I do not remember to have seen more than two of the natives. There were a man and a woman who availed of our steamer to go up the country. These were of a distinctly yellow colour, with tolerably regular features and long black hair. The female wore a loose calico gown with a small shawl, worn sometimes on the head, sometimes on the shoulders. Of the man I do not recollect anything in particular. They were about the medium height of Europeans.

As far as was visible from the steamer and the place we landed at, the country appeared to be almost uninhabited along the course of the San Juan. The scenery was very interesting. The ground sloped up from the river in most places, forming as the landscape expanded and receded a most beautiful panorama of hills and mountains – innumerable peaks and pinnacles gradually rising higher and higher till in the distance the great mountain tops lost themselves in the clouds. It was about the second half of March and the first of April. The temperature was generally 80° with a humid atmosphere. The vegetation was very dense as far as the eye could reach. It appeared to be of a kind that had resulted from neglect, due possibly to the unsettled conditions of the country.

Heavy timber did not lie near to the river – but a rank tropical vegetation, the growth of possibly six or more years, covered everything to
the water's edge.

In some places where we landed we did see trees of considerable size,
but these places had the least uncivilized of what I saw – for in those
places were to be seen fruit trees: lemons, oranges, bananas, peppers,
etc. Probably such places had been more recently abandoned.

We came upon several abandoned native dwellings. They were of a
very primitive kind – a roof supported on strong posts, having on one
side a slight protection. Covered up with coarse matting or rough
planks, no fire place. The fire was evidently made up outside the house.

Indeed, in New Orleans, in the most humble dwellings that came
under my observations the cooking was carried on in a building
separated from the dwelling or with a bucket-like stove in the open yard
of the house.

In the course of the river were sandbanks rising above the surface of
the water, possibly those were in the lower part of the river and were
regularly covered by sea tides, or they had been formed during the rainy
season and were left uncovered during the dry season. But what attracted
my attention to those sand banks were the great patches covered with
what appeared to be flowers of the most brilliant and dazzling colours.
On one occasion I was able to get upon of those sand banks, and making
straight for my bed of flowers, they took flight and resolved into a moving
mass of butterflies which were soon out of my reach. They were at least
four times as large as the butterflies to be found in Ireland. I have never
seen elsewhere butterflies so large and gorgeously coloured.

Walker appeared to have possession of the valley of the San Juan. For
as we advanced up the river we found supplies of wood prepared at
intervals for fuel for our steam boat. At some places however precautions
were taken: by throwing and scouts were thrown out to prevent a surprise
attack. A few shots were occasionally exchanged, but with no result.

At length after about a month of this deliberate progress we
approached Fort San Carlos at the entrance to Lake Nicaragua and after
a halt we advanced to attack it. We approached so closely to it that I
heard those in the fort talking quite distinctly. I did not understand

Spanish and so did not know what they said. They were strengthening their position by cutting down the timber which was pretty thick around there.

Amongst the foul-tongued in our crowd was a young insignificant looking fellow. As we advanced to attack the fort I noticed the chap pale and quiet, reading a pocket bible.

There was, however, no attack. When we arrived at the fort a parley ensued and it was found that dispatches were there from Walker notifying that he had made terms of peace and agreed to retire from the country. Like the King of France, who with his men 'marched up the hill' and then marched down again – we having marched up the hill (on which Fort San Carlos was situated) now marched down again. In leisurely manner we returned to the place where we left our steamer. We found there a second steamboat. Ours was built of wood, this new one was of iron.

I do not remember how many days we spent on our return voyage down the river. We had accomplished the greater part of our return voyage when the following incident took place. The wooden steamboat, having on board the leading men of the party – among them General Wheat – a big man about 6ft 2in and some 16 stone in weight – was in advance of the iron boat. Many of us were enjoying a foot bath: sitting on the side of the boat, which was low in the water, our feet were in the water. In this luxurious situation we were disturbed by a loud noise and cries from the other steamer which was about 100 yards ahead of us. We saw she was enveloped in a cloud of steam, overtopping which I observed the boat's hurricane deck upon which was the big man Wheat.

The deck fell into the river from a height of some 30 to 50 feet, and my brave Wheat, freeing himself from the wreck of the hurricane deck, stood up, the river at that place was about 4 feet deep. He shook himself like a water dog and walked ashore unhurt – I suppose the hurricane deck saved him from the effects of the steam. The bow of the steamboat, when the explosion took place, had just struck a sand bank. Those on board landed on to the sandback as quickly as possible.

With the exception of three, all were unhurt. These three were severely scalded. They were made as comfortable as possible on to the sandbank, from which I gather that it was not a tidal position of the river, and the necessary dressing was promptly applied. I had with me one or two white calico shirts and I gave them up for the benefit of those poor sufferers.

The wooden steamboat having thus been disabled the remainder of the journey to the Sea of San Juan was accomplished by the small iron boat in several trips. I think our party must have been joined at San Carlos by some who had come from the Pacific side of the country, for on our return were some persons whom I had not noticed before.

I may have been too general and sweeping in my descriptions of those who composed this expedition. There were among them a half-dozen or more with whom, as far as I was able to judge, I would not be ashamed to be seen in civilised society.

In due time – as one of the first draft of the iron steamboat – I reached San Juan. Where I learned that those who composed the expedition were to be brought to the mouth of the Mississippi on board British ships of war. San Juan was then in the possession of the Commanders of these ships. And on entering the town we were required to give up our arms – to be returned when disembarking at New Orleans. Some managed to retain their revolvers. I can now (25/12/95) recollect with what relish I feasted that day in San Juan on a box of sardines, a bottle of Bass Ale and biscuits.

On one of those days I was reclining on a bench in a corner of the coffee house in which I had had my feast of sardines, biscuits and ale, when in came six of the leading men of the expedition. General Wheat, before referred to, Col. Anderson, Col. Lockwood, a brother of General Walker and others whose names I did not know. They had a drink all around, but it appeared that among them they had not as much as would discharge the reckoning. General Wheat, espying me in the corner, came over and asked me to lend him thirty-three cents. I unbuttoned my pocket (I had adopted that measure of precaution) and was about giving him the money, but apparently not with that alacrity he desired for he made use of some offensive language. Whereupon I buttoned my pocket saying, 'You are not going to get it now.'

Wheat stopped to strike me – I was reclining on the bench. I put up my feet and gave him a smart kick in the stomach or chest – which drove him back from me. I jumped to my feet and twirling around my head a [whalebone?] cane with leaded head and was about to strike him with the heavy end of it when I saw Colonel Anderson aiming at me with a revolver. The ruffians were nearly or wholly drunk and fortunately the door was beside me. I bolted pretty nimbly.

General Walker's brother was the first to reach the door after me. The only weapon he had was I suppose a bowie knife, which he flung at me, but it fell short. The effort, however, too much for his then unstable equilibrium and he fell forward on face and hands.

I had no difficulty outrunning men in their condition. But finding that they continued to follow me and observing the British flag flying from the usual staff beside a house within easy reach I judged this to be the residence of the British Consul. In this unpleasant and dangerous predicament I began to consider what I ought to do.

The idea of seeking the protection of the British Consul (his name I found was Green) and the British flag was hateful to me, but I could see no other way out of the difficulty for San Juan contained but a few houses widely scattered.

I decided that under the circumstances it was my duty to submit to this humiliation, the greatest of my whole life.

So, full of pain and indignation I made for the accursed flag.

The Consul's house was of one story solidly built. A flight of steps with a coping at each side led up to it. It was enclosed by a low wall, through which an iron gate gave admittance. I was some 150 yards in advance of my pursuers – so I was able to approach the Consul's house deliberately. I rang the house bell. Mr Green's name was on a brass place on the door. Mr Green himself opened the door and stepped outside to me.

I explained my position – showed him the men who were pursuing me – told him I was an Irishman, and demanded protection.

My pursuers soon came up, and they gathered outside the wall, which separated the Consul's ground from the road. This wall being no more than fifty feet or so from the house they were within speaking distance, and they hurled a lot of abusive language at me for about an hour. The Consul warned them a few times and finally they disappeared.

We were to embark the next day so that I had to avoid those men for only one night and that night I slept on the sea shore wrapped up in my blanket – the wash of the tide, which was very gentle, serving for my lullaby. Next day we were carried on board the British ship of war. I do not remember the ship's name. I think she was the 'Tiger'. Our voyage to the mouth of the Mississippi was uneventful.

There, while waiting for steamboats to take us up the river to New Orleans, about 48 hours I think, I witnessed the grandest storm of rain, thunder and lightning I have ever seen.

During that time the rain fell in such quantities that there was all the time about three inches of water on the ship's deck. The thunder and lightning behaved in such a way that on two occasions I really thought that the ship's guns were being discharged. The lightning flamed all around. The ship shook and quivered as if from the recoil of the guns. This terrific storm passed. In perhaps a quarter of an hour after the storm ceased a general sunshine made everything delightful.

The steamboats had come alongside the ordinary tug boats which were carrying ships up to New Orleans – and we quickly transferred ourselves and our belongings.

On the way up I entered into chat with an old Pole as I then felt inclined to describe him, but whom I would now call a middle-aged man (he was about fifty years old). I had not met him before.

He had, according to his own account, been engaged in some insurrectionary movement at home. Escaping from the clutches of the Russians, he had joined the French Foreign Legion and having come to America had joined one of the expeditions to Nicaragua. I was glad to be in a position to contribute a little towards his immediate necessities.

On arriving at New Orleans I went at once to Mrs Connolly's boarding house where I had left my luggage. As soon as I had made myself presentable I called on Joe Brennan. It was with sincere regret that I found him confined to bed in a low state of health.

He welcomed me most warmly. And when I had told him a little of my experiences in Nicaragua he requested me – there and then, to sit down and put on paper what I had to say.

Brennan had during my absence started a newspaper, of his own, and, as fast as I filled each sheet of paper it was carried off to the office of the journal (*The Times*, I think it was called). I think they issued six extra editions of the journal containing my descriptions of what I had seen.

I do not think that Brennan was ever able to work again. As well as I can recall, he lingered for but a short time. Like Williams he left a widow with two children. Mrs Brennan with her children soon went North to her brother John Savage who I believe was in good circumstances.

Chapter 4

In New Orleans before the War, 1857–1861

After my return from Nicaragua I had some idea of taking a voyage to Calcutta; but before deciding determined to visit an old political friend Dalton Williams who was teaching school at Baton Rouge, 89 miles above New Orleans. The population was then but 4,000, yet there meets the legislature of the state of Louisiana, there are the state buildings and offices in connection therewith. It is the custom in the United States to select as state capital the most central not necessarily the most important city.

Having made a few journeys on the river steamboats, to and from Baton Rouge and New Orleans, also to and from Plaquemine, perhaps a few words' description of the steamboats will not be amiss.

Some of the largest were more than 300 feet long. The machinery was contained in the hull. The deck extended about one foot beyond the hull – thus increasing the space for cargo – and I day say also increasing the stability of the vessel.

The passengers were accommodated on the second deck, which stood about eight feet above the cargo deck; the second deck was approached by two stairs. With the exception of some twenty to twenty-five fore and oft reserved for lounging and promenading the deck was occupied by passenger cabins and saloons.

The passenger cabins outside – the saloons running down between the cabins. The fore saloon was the dining and general saloon – about two-thirds of the length – the other third was the Ladies' Saloon. On the large boats I think there was a passage on each side – outside the passengers cabins.

During fine weather, which generally prevailed, that portion of this deck which extended from the saloons etc towards the bow was usually occupied by smokers and talkers. It was the favourite lounge.

The cargoes of these boats mostly consisted of cotton bales – in shape [of] oblong cubes, were piled up, presenting the appearance of a solid wall of cotton bales all around the cargo deck. The great sugar hogsheads, corn (in bags), etc in the centre of the deck.[1]

The appearance of these boats, the better class especially, was pleasing. They were usually painted white and in the clear sunny atmosphere they looked like floating palaces. But, lit up at night, they were fair palaces, and with music on board the effect was most pleasing.

The interior decorating of the saloons was very attractive – generally white and gold – with a liberal display of mirrors.

Gamblers were ever on the watch for victims on these boats and many an unfortunate is taken in the toil – an occasional brawl resulting from time to time – not always bloodless.

As on the Atlantic traffic there are champion liners – so the Mississippi also had its crack steamboats – 'The Empire State' was the last built, the largest and the finest boat at the time I write of.[2] Not infrequently two crack boats would time their starting so as to have a trial of speed on the voyage up or down the river. On some occasions the excitement went high indeed – in the height of the contest the rival captains have not hesitated to convert portions of the cargoes into fuel rather than stop at the usual stations for supplies of wood. Of course races of this kind are not without danger – and terrible consequences have at times resulted. I do not know whether they have within the past thirty-three years been prohibited.

Landing at Plaquemine on the way to Baton Rouge a friend proposed to take me out in his buggy and show me the Highlands. I accepted with pleasure – the sight of the 'highlands' would be a welcome relief after the long stretch of dead level country I had seen. When we had driven as far as I thought the highlands ought to be, according to my friend's description, I asked him, 'By the way, where are the Highlands?' 'We have passed them,' he replied. 'I will point them out as we return.' On our return I was resolved that they should not escape us.

If I had been driving over the same road for twenty years, if I had not been informed about the Highlands, I don't think I should have ever discovered them. What was called a name so well calculated to arouse enthusiasm in a very flat country was a slight indulation in the surface – the road dipped down some six or eight feet, ascending again perhaps twelve feet.

I do not know whether the name was given in mockery. I know it disgusted me.

When I landed from the steamboat I went at once to hunt up Williams. I had never seen the gentleman up to this time.

He was one of the band of '48 men of whom Ireland is still proud. He was better known to the Irish Nationalist public as 'Shamrock of the *Nation*'. He had been for some years contributing to its pages short poems which were keenly appreciated.

He had been also, I think, connected with either the *Tribune* or the *Felon* newspaper. I believe the [illegible]. If I do not mistake he had to promise to leave Ireland before he was released from prison. At all events he did go to America on his release.[3]

I think Williams had been informed by some member of his wife's family that I was about to visit him. At all events I presented myself before him without delay. I found him with his class – about eight boys – around him, he apparently entertaining them with some interesting description, they chalking his back!

Williams appeared to be under forty years – height about 5ft 6in, fair complexion, beard and also fair, the latter rather long, face rather round, features regular. His sight was evidently weak and he wore glasses.

Poor Shamrock! He was very amiable and good tempered, full of anecdotes. A most enjoyable companion.

He gave me some account of himself since he arrived in America. I suppose it was at New York he first landed. He had a little money, which he knew would not keep him long. So he endeavoured to obtain employment of some sort through those to whom he had been introduced. I believe he did get some trifling temporary jobs, but he had quite run down financially when one day one of those who had been trying to help him came to tell him that there was an opening as clerk to a merchant who was visiting some of the southern cities with a view to selling his good there. The thought of Williams in such a position was simply laughable. But he was ready to turn his had to anything for a living.

He was a medical student and I was surprised that he did not follow his profession! I suppose it was not congenial – he was a literary man more than anything else – he was a poet and journalist. He was however a mere child in the ways of the world – and entirely unable to help himself and for commercial purposes he must have been quite useless.

Yet perhaps the Yankee cheap jack saw the manifest guileless innocence of Williams could be made useful. For who could suspect roguery in connection with a man of such transparent honesty. They visited several of the southern cities on this business tour. I forget the name of the city where it concluded, perhaps Savannah in Georgia.

They sold out the last of the stock and the proprietor 'went back to the North' to prepare a fresh supply – leaving Williams in charge of the store in which the sales were held.

Either the next day or possibly a day or two later Williams was trying to kill time reading the newspapers in the store when he noticed a number of persons approaching the store. He described them as having the appearance of indignant citizens. They came and crowded around the store.

Immediately they began to denounce and abuse poor Williams as a cheat and a rogue. And from words they quickly proceed to hustle and knock him about. He was in absolute danger at the hands of those men when by some good fortune an Irishman in the crowd caught some idea of who he was – and explanations were entered into. It appeared that the dealer in Yankee notions had so grossly imposed upon the purchasers of the goods. And that poor Williams was in complete ignorance of the man's character and that there never was a more innocent accomplice and decoy.

I think Lynch was the name of the Irishman who came to Williams's rescue. He completely turned the tables, and those who a short time before had intentions of lynching Williams, when the explanations had been made united in welcoming him and fêting him.

For this place he after a while drifted farther south, to the college of Springfield near Mobile in the state of Alabama. There he remained for several years as professor of English Literature. I suppose he got tired of this sort of life. He at all events left Springfield and – by what stage, I do not remember, if I ever heard – he drifted to New Orleans and lived at Mrs Connolly's Boarding House in Julia St. This I merely presume as explaining his marriage with Miss Connolly – and they on to Baton Rouge were I found him teaching school for the Jesuits who were in charge of the mission there.

I soon learned that Williams was then on the eve of leaving. I believe he was waiting only that the Fathers might find a substitute to carry on the school.

When I found that Father Lavay (I am not certain that I write name correctly – he was French and I spell the name as it was pronounced) the superior was quite distressed about the school, without any consideration or hesitation I offered to take up the work – without charge beyond my keep – until he should procure a teacher.

My offer was accepted on the spot. Before entering upon my experiences of school teaching I think it better fellow the fortunes of poor lovable 'Shamrock.' I do not think we met again for about four years. He had been most of this time teaching at a few places within easy reach of New Orleans, so he occasionally visited that city. I may have met him during one or more of those visits to New Orleans. It is quite likely that I did.

But in 1862 he spent some days in the city and I learned with great regret that his health had become very bad – that he had had more than one attack of haemorrhage of the lungs. He told me that his doctor warned him that another attack might prove fatal. The poor fellow was in no way troubled about this, for *himself*. He felt the battle of life had been too much for him and he would not regret laying down the burden and giving up the fight.

He did feel troubled for his wife and two young children whom he should leave unprovided. He dined with me the day before he had fixed up for returning to the scene of his labour in Thibodeauxville or Ibberville I think it was.[4] He appeared to put all care aside, and was as gay and cheerful and as full of anecdote as ever. He did not worry about things – as I could not have helped doing under like circumstances. We spent a very pleasant evening at my humble dwelling in Good Children St, or Rue des Bons Enfants, 3rd district.

A fortnight after he was dead aged 39. After the capture of New Orleans by Admiral Farragut the Federal Troops went through the state of Louisiana. A body of them was temporarily stationed at the place where poor 'Shamrock' died – many of them were Irishmen to whom the nom de plume was well known and loved.

Before they left the place these loving exiles had a nice tomb erected to the self-sacrificing patriot who had practically lost all for Ireland's sake.

God bless the warm hearted exiles.

And as for Richard D'Alton Williams,

     Requiest in pace.

I took up the baton and [illegible] laid down by poor Williams.

A good sized house was rented for me by the Jesuit Fathers, with large rooms on the ground floor – suitable for school rooms. One a bed room was furnished for me and one of the large rooms was fitted up with benches and desks. It was a more pretentious house than that Williams had.

After consultation with Father Lavay I issued quite an imposing prospectus, and of course he and Father Prachkinski, the other Jesuit who belonged to the Mission, whipped up amongst the members of the congregations for scholars.

I threw myself into the work, and in a short time had a fairly good number of pupils, which gradually increased to thirty. I had one pupil, a young man of about 18 years of age. His father, named Prendergast, was well to do, carrying on business in the town. He was [a] dull young fellow. To make a favourable impression I devoted much time and trouble to this pupil (he came to me after school hours). The result that before I left was that he told me he had never learned anything but what he learned from me.

I was prouder of the following little incident than of many others of greater importance affecting myself. My rule was that any boy whose work was badly done should remain after school hours to make up the lesson in which he had been deficient. One day I told a boy that he was marked for this discipline. The pupils went to dinner about midday and returned for another few hours. This boy did not return after dinner. The other boys saw that I was displeased, and when school was dismissed a number of them, without giving me any hint of what they intended, went to that boy's house and brought him to me (carrying him neck and heels to me).

I was one day sitting on the door steps of my school house one Sunday after my arrival. I observed quite a crowd – perhaps 200 –negroes coming out of a small place of worship – Baptist I think. They passed me by so that I had a good opportunity of noting them.

About an equal number of males and females – they were all comfortably and cleanly dressed – many black coats, high top hats, silver headed canes, watch chains among the men. The women were dressed mostly in muslins, and some carried fans and parasols. There was no one near me at the time of whom to ask questions.

I have heard that there were quite a number of free negroes ('coloured people', they were called) in Louisiana and I concluded that the crowd I saw were of this class. But to my astonishment I learned that they were slaves, belonging to the neighbouring plantations.

As far as my observations went, they appeared to be the happiest and most comfortable labouring people I had ever seen before or have since seen.

Before leaving Ireland I met a friend who had been in America and made some stay in the slave states. He spoke about the condition of the slaves as he saw it. He was almost defending the Institutions of slavery and I could not tolerate any word of excuse or defence and I condemned, in the strongest languages, the whole system – root and branch.

The reason I have not mentioned the name of the father of my grown-up pupil is that I learned this of him. He was the father of a young girl whose mother was his slave. I have seen this girl more than once. She was almost white – I would not have known she was not white if I had not been told otherwise. This man (Irish I regret to say) kept this girl in slavery, and I was told that the girl had been flogged more than once, for what offence or on what pretence I do not remember.

During my intimate relations with the Jesuit Fathers at Baton Rouge – continued subsequently at New Orleans – and as far as visiting

occasionally, I learned the following estimate of the different nation-
alities from one special point of view.

– On receiving a sick call from an Irishman there is no necessity for
haste. It is not likely to be a case of urgency, of the Irishman's first idea
in case of a hurt or an illness of any kind was to send for the priest.
– If the sick call be from a Belgian it might be treated almost as that
from an Irishman, but with a little more promptitude.
– If from a German, no necessary delay should be made.
– If from a Spaniard, about the same as the German.
– But on receiving a sick call from a Frenchman or an Italian – rush
away at once or the man will be dead before you can arrive.

One afternoon, while I was having supper with the Jesuits at Baton
Rouge (as was my custom, so long as I remained at Baton Rouge), Father
Lavay was summoned to the church to tie the nuptial knot for a couple.
He returned to the supper table after the marriage, and he produced the
paper of *confitures* (in which the French were accustomed to wrap up
the sum of money, their sense of the proprieties would not permit them
to hand to the priest openly).[5] And having opened the little package, it
was found to contain about half penny worth of sweets but no money! I
was sorry to learn that this was not an entirely new experience.

The dining room of the Jesuit Fathers at Baton Rouge was modest in
every respect – as to furniture, size etc. In the warm weather, which
prevailed at the time I am writing of, the door which opened into the
chapel yard (to which there was of course free admission from the road
or street) was left fully open – so that a person from outside could easily
see those sitting at the table. The supper hour was after nightfall.

One afternoon while the two priests sat at table a shot was fired at
Father Lavay. The bullet struck his arm which happened to be in front
of his breast – I think one or both bones of the arm were broken. It was
thought the bullet would have entered the heart but that the arm
happened to be in such a position.

Having spent four months as a teacher at Baton Rouge, and having,
in my own opinion at least, put the school into a creditable state, I made

up my mind that I should not care to act the pedagogue any longer, and I went down to New Orleans intending to look for an opening in the commercial world.

As New Orleans became my home for some years it is perhaps proper I should say something concerning its somewhat [illegible] situation and arrangements. But I might as well now state briefly the impression made upon me, as I ascended the river five or six months later, on my return from Nicaragua.

The extreme end, where the river meets the sea, is mud. Very soon you observe coarse reeds springing up in swampy land, quite as much water as land, for I do not think that for miles one could safely rest a foot upon it. Gradually the surface becomes more closely covered with vegetation. As you continue to ascend, the surface appears to become more solid. Low brushwood shows higher and then wood and forests come in to view and New Orleans appears at 109 miles from the mouth of the river.

The Levée however is something more than the landing place for ships – I am now describing only that portion of which is appropriated to shipping, loading and unloading. This timber quay runs along the river frontage of the city for miles. In places it was extending 100 yards of more from the bank in the river and consequently it afforded large accommodation for depositing thereon the merchandise discharged or about to be loaded.

Of course a great proportion of the cotton, sugar, Indian corn, and tobacco which was brought to New Orleans in the great river steamers was intended for exportation. And this merchandise was removed from the steamboats to the ships' loading place and piled up covered with tarpaulin while waiting for the ship to arrive.

In like manner the bulk of the cargoes brought by the ships was destined for the cities and towns higher up the Mississippi and its great tributaries, and such goods would wait the arrival of the steamboats.

The steamboats, being of light draft, could come close to the bank, and did not need the accommodation of the timer built portion of the levée – these had a separate landing place.

The levée properly so called is a great bank of earth – and earthwork built up to save the low lying land from the waters of the great river, which in the spring season attain a height much above the level of New Orleans and the country below it and above it for many miles. At this season the tributaries of the Mississippi are swollen with the melted snow from the mountains and highlands of the many thousands of miles of country drained by them. And as a consequence the big river rises to a great height as it flows past New Orleans. Looking back now I should say that opposite the city the earthwork rises 20 or 30 feet – is about 20 or 30 feet broad at the top and perhaps 150 feet at the base.

Before slavery was abolished each planter was bound to keep in order that portion of the levée beside his plantation. He had also to attend to such roads as ran through his lands – this attention was not much; it was merely levelling the surface and filling up the big ruts cut into the earth by traffic, which was in many places very small.

Of course where various plantations were concerned all would combine – or the parish authority would come into action. If a portion of this good earthwork became weakened through neglect or some mishap the swollen river would break through. This was a revasse, and if not quickly attended to and the injury made good the most dreadful consequences might follow – the country would be inundated and laid waste far and wide.

It has taken us quite a long time to cross the levée and enter the city. The weather was beautiful on the day I landed – the sky was a clear blue without a cloud, the sun so warm an alpaca coat was quite heavy enough.

Canal Street – the chief street of New Orleans – begins near the levée where ships lie and runs back to the country. It contains many of the best shops (called stores). Through the middle of it formerly ran a canal, I think it was but a large drain to carry off the water from swampy ground lying back of the city. This canal had been covered over years 1857 – but where it ran farther back than the street extended it was still open in 1857 and up to 1862.

Canal Street divided the city into two halves – each half contained two districts. Going from Canal Street up parallel with the river you pass through the first district and higher up was the fourth district. The third district was the extreme south while the fourth was the north end of the city, supposing the course of the river in front of New Orleans to be from north to south.

Canal Street is very wide. The centre of it, called the neutral ground, had a double row of trees and was a shady promenade. Each side of the street had a very wide, flagged footway. And between each footway and the neutral ground was a roadway. Canal Street in my time was comparatively new. Earlier the best shops were in Royal St and Dauphin St in the second district. The first district contained the bulk of the Native Americans.

The second district was largely French. The third district was also largely French but there were also many of the old Spanish families – for Louisiana had been a Spanish colony before it became French.

The greater part of the Irish also were to be found in the third district. And in the fourth district were the Germans. There were exceptions to the above distribution. For there was a considerable number of Irish to be found in the German quarter and in the American quarter.

The archbishopal palace, erected in 1737, was the oldest building in the city. The Cathedral of St Louis was a fine gothic structure. The Custom House, a striking building, was completed about a year after my arrival. I was told that to secure a safe foundation was almost a greater work than the erection of the building, that the piling was a very heavy work and that there was more work under the surface than above it.

The private dwellings of the wealthy business people extended for some miles by the river beyond the fourth district or North side of the city. There were almost all frame built and were stood some three feet above the soil. Heavy beams were laid on support of brick or stone, the supports rising about three feet above ground – and on those beams the house was built. They were in some instances weather-boarded. Painted white generally, the persiennes painted green.[6] In the suburbs the houses had in most instances verandahs around three sides. The houses were all detached – standing in nicely trimmed gardens – with creepers trained over the verandahs. Multitudes of flowering shrubs, orange trees with their golden fruit, and stately magnolias – the flowers of which gave out a rich perfume which was almost overpowering – made a delightful scene.

Before going to America I had read of houses being moved from one place to another. In New Orleans I saw one instance of this: it was a

small two storey house. Strong chains were secured about the frame –
timbers – a powerful team of many horses was employed to put it in
motion. It was very slowly moved on rollers and was successfully
removed about 200 yards.

The cemetery of New Orleans presented a strange aspect in the
burial places of the various benevolent societies. Belonging to each
Society was what appeared to be a number of ovens arranged in three
tiers – but apparent oven was a vault closed with an iron door. It was
only the poorest were buried in the earth (if it can be described). I saw
such a grave dug out and it was nearly full of water – the water being
found at a depth of 6 inches. The better off people had their tombs or
vaults constructed above ground – some of these were costly and
sculptured more or less richly.

The drainage of the city was of a rather primitive kind – surface
cuttings or small canals carrying the superfluous water away into the
swamps. A bad system, one would think, since it was calculated to keep
the swamp almost up to the doors of the city. But this bad system was
neglected: the water courses were not kept clear.[7]

The summer temperature was ordinarily about 80° but it often was
84° and 85° while during a regular hot spell it went up as high as 95°. The
summer was certainly enervating. I remember an edition of the *True Delta*
newspaper (owned and edited by an Irishman named John McGuinness)
which was issued during a hot spell in which the editor expressed the
fervent wish that he could lay aside the flesh and sit in his bones to cool
himself. It was decidedly not easy to work hard with the thermometer
at 90°.

It was common to see men going home from business in the afternoons, having coat on arm and hat in hand. I have usually or at least
frequently done so in warm weather. There was more 'free and easy' in
New Orleans than I have seen elsewhere. In quiet and retired parts of
the city when the house stood on the banquette (footway) you might
have seen members of a family taking tea or other refreshment on the
banquette: I have often enjoyed my smoke and glass of wine or grog
alfresco in this fashion in my shirt sleeves. I was never in any place where
people troubled so little about what their neighbour thought.[8]

If there by any place where the redoubtable and odious Mrs Grundy is unknown I would say that at the time I write of she was not known in New Orleans.

The civic government was I fear very corrupt. Frightful stories were told something with no bated breath in the newspapers – of corruptions of the most alarming kind.

It was openly stated the chief Police Officer (I forget what he was called) had committed at least two murders. A mysterious and daring murder was committed and a very public street (Canal St., I think), a place supposed to be well patrolled by police. No clue was ever reported by the police – but the newspapers boldly stated that the murder was done by the police, and that in most cases the perpetrators of undiscovered murders would be found in the ranks of the police.[9]

I have seen Canal Street, the principal street of the city, covered with water, more than two feet in part, after a heavy fall of rain. In three hours the water had disappeared leaving a coating of mud. And in another hour or two this mud was blowing about as dust.

It is easy to believe that the low situation of the city and the nearness of the swamp was largely accountable for its unfavourable hygienic conditions – and the condition naturally becomes worse when the watercourses are allowed to become choked with mud and weeds.

It is only right to say that I was informed that General Butler devoted attention to the city drainage and the swamp into which they carried the water. In my experience, from February 1857 to October 1862, New Orleans was twice visited by yellow fever, and suffered severely each time.

Before the civil war the usual thing was for people in good circumstances to go away in April, returning in September or October.

During my sojourn at Baton Rouge I was attacked by what was called an acclimating fever, which must have been something akin to yellow fever. It continued for 48 hours after which I found the sickness had left me. But on attempting to leave the bed I found myself unable to stand, even though supporting myself by the bed, and it was with difficulty I succeeded in getting back into the bed – so much had the fever weakened me in that short time. That was the only illness I had while in America.

As I have referred to the summer temperature to I ought to say a word about the winter.

A fire was always agreeable in the evening. I once saw the street powdered as it were with flour. This was the one specimen of snow in my experience. It might have been the same winter – but of this I am not clear – when I saw a very thin ice on water pools. I saw no other sign of frost.

I have experience[d] gloomy days in winter with sometimes a sharp wind – and occasionally a cold rain – which was most disagreeable. But generally the winter was rather enjoyable.

During summer the mosquitoes were very troublesome. They have strung me though my (prunella) boots and through my trousers (their material of course).[10] Those who are acclimated do not trouble about them except in summer. But I remember my first night in New Orleans, February 1st, the steward neglected to arrange the mosquito bar of my bed. I had had a fatiguing day and I slept rather heavily. In the morning a large number of hitherto unsuspected bumps were quite visible on my cranium. That was my first experience of those pests. I had previously no knowledge of the mosquito bar – but I never forgot while I was exposed to the attack of that relentless and insatiable foe, before attempting to settle myself in my bed, I was careful to have the bar properly drawn, making a careful examination lest one or more of the enemy might during the day or the previous night have penetrated through the meshes of the net of which the mosquito bar was made. If I discovered one or more I at once attacked them with a fan or a towel and ceased till I had driven him out.

The mosquitoes were a terror at night – the thin shrill hum of one of the rascals would make me ever so uncomfortable until I had satisfied myself that he was not inside the bar.

I suppose I ought to describe what the bar was. It was made of net – a coarse, sufficiently fine mesh to prevent the passage of those small plagues. It was hung, with rings, upon iron or brass rods attached to the roof of the four-post bedstead. It had a top of calico corresponding in size to the square roof of the bed – the net formed four sides corresponding with sides of the bed – falling down loosely. When not in use it was drawn – the rings rimming the rods – to the end of the bed. At night it was expanded so as to fall closely around the bed leaving a clear space for the expectant sleeper, within which he might hope to enjoy nature's sweet restorer – provided none of the enemy had by any chance made an entry – and provided there was no defect in the net through which to effect a lodgement.

One of the great sights of New Orleans was the Fire Brigade.

What a display it made on every fête day! The greatest festival was Washington's Day – the 8th February, I think. On that day the Fire Brigade turned out in all its bravery – every engine and every machine of every description burnished and brightened to the highest pitch, and everything magnificently decorated with flowers of the richest and rarest procurable. And of course the ranks of the firemen were on this day at their fullest.

This needs a little explanation. For many reasons jury service was avoided and evaded by all possible means by business men. The Firemen were excused from this service and consequently nearly every man in business – merchants, shopkeepers and traders of all sorts – joined the Fire Brigade Corps – of which there were many scattered about the city. Very few of these men did duty as Firemen beyond turning out on the big shows – in themselves occasions for gaining popularity for those big merchants – who possibly might have an eye to a future political advantage. (But if the merchants and traders did not attend fires they contributed to the funds of corps to which they belonged).

It, of course, goes without saying that the turn out on Washington's birthday was not confined to the Fire Brigade. Every trade and society, every handicraft, made the best show possible, on those occasions – with bands, banners, decorations, specimens of their work and insignia, etc. But the Fire Brigade headed the parade and was the leading item in it in every respect.

When the special privileges were conferred on the Fire Brigade it was evidently in order to attract men to it. At that time the city was to a greater extent than it was at the time I write of (1857–62) built of wood, and owing to dry, warm climate those wooden houses were like so much tinder and of course fires were terribly destructive.

Even in my time the 2nd and 3rd districts, the latter especially, contained many wooden houses; the Cotton Presses – where
immense quantities of cotton were repackaged – were also at the end of
the 3rd district.

I remember one terrible fire among those cotton presses – which
devastated them – destroying a great quantity of cotton – and swept
bare a large extent of the surrounding and neighbouring streets. But for
the district in which the fire had broken out was quickly known
according as the firebell tolled a regular intervals, one, two, three or four,
'one' being of course 1st district, 'two' 2nd district, and so on.

As this fire bell rang the warning was taken up by each corps until the
whole city was filled by the clamour of the bells. Then a sight would be
seen: men rushing from every side of the engines, the hose ready, hook
and ladder wagons dashed along the streets.

Some men apparently kept their helmets and coats in their homes
while others had to run to the Engine Houses for them. For you would
see them rushing out of workshops and out of the houses thrusting their
arms into the coat sleeves – helmets hanging by the chains as the ran –
they jumped upon an omnibus or tram car when such happened to serve
– some took cabs but every man got to the fire as rapidly as possible.

Thirty-five years ago the Fire Brigade was the greatest institution in
New Orleans.

To Irish Catholics the following brief account of the religious organisation of the Germans in New Orleans will appear strange. I think I
have said that the Germans were almost all to be found in the 4th district.
They had their own schools and their own church as well as I remember
in one block of buildings, well built. A committee managed church and
schools, and paid priest and teachers. Some of the Redemptorist Fathers
attended the church – I think they had a residence adjoining it. I did not
like the system of lay management.

So much for the general appearance of the city and its climate.

Through Joe Brennan I got to know a Mr M. J. Brennan who was
engaged in Wholesale Provision trade in partnership with a Mr Place,
and through M J Brennan I became acquainted with a Mr Kingsland and
others in the same trade. I used to call at the offices of these gentlemen

occasionally – chat and read the papers. Kingsland always received me very kindly.

The necessity of doing something for a living now becoming urgent, I was for sometime trying to screw up my courage to take some sort of decisive step with this object – but being very shy (perhaps it was a ridiculous pride) I found it difficult to take this first step. At length I one day asked Kingsland to allow me to assist him in his office work – I said something to this effect: that if he would confer a favour upon me by affording me an opportunity for gaining experience and getting my hand in – and that of course I should not expect payment.

To this request he complied in the kindest way – and I set to work at once.

At the end of one month he said he would now allow me twenty dollars a month, with which I was well pleased, and I felt that I should get along steadily. At the end of the second month he gave me, not the twenty dollars he had promised, but twenty-five for the past month – and another twenty-five for the first month. He said very kindly that I was worth more and if he was in need of my services, if his business permitted it, he would pay me better.

I think it was only at the end of the third month he advanced my salary to fifty dollars a month. When I made his acquaintance I think he had but recently started in business on his own account. His trade was very moderate, I suppose it was not a success, for when I had been five months with him he told me he was about to get out of business. At this time the firm of Place and Brennan was winding up – the term of partnership and their bookkeeper having left them. I was asked to take his place while the business was being wound up.

This was a great advantage to me in more ways than one: I had never before seen a regular set of books, and having now got this opportunity I made a regular study of the work – I bought the best book on book-keeping I could get – and when the work was completed at this house I had qualified as a regular bookkeeper and I was able to refer to those whose business I had wound up.

After a month of so I made an engagement at $1000 a year – and in a year or two I gave this up for another at $1200 – when I got a partnership which under ordinary circumstances would be worth between $2,000 and $3,000 a year.

I was now on the high road to fortune when everything went down before the war storm which for a considerable time had been brewing.

I had got married a few years before this and had now two children (a stepson and my own son) as well as a wife to provide for. My wife had been the widow of a young man named Patrick O'Brien, a native of Waterford City. I met him and his wife at the boarding house at which I had been living. The yellow fever was very bad the following summer and it carried off poor O'Brien and the widow was left in straightened circumstances.

When I had settled down to work in New Orleans and was able to make a living one of my very first thoughts was – to find out whether any work was being done for Ireland with the desire to take a part in it.

I heard nothing on this subject from Williams nor from Brennan. Indeed I think Brennan had died before the time I am referring to: the latter part of 1857. The only prominent Irishman in the States of whom much had been heard about this time or rather earlier, was John Mitchel. After turning the matter over in my mind I decided to write him – I think he was then living in Tennessee.

I did write him stating briefly what I wanted to know and the reason why. By way of introduction I sent him a letter I had received from John Martin. In due time I received Mitchel's reply, advising me to attend to my own business and cease troubling about Ireland! Such an advice – and from John Mitchel – shocked and grieved me – but did not influence or affect me otherwise.

I had already observed on the part of Smith O'Brien – when he had been permitted to return to Ireland a few years earlier – a disposition to condemn the spirit of unrest (new aspirations had not I think yet begun to take shape) which was occasionally manifested in the country.

Chapter 5

In New Orleans after the War, 1861–1862

From the time of my arrival in New Orleans I was greatly struck with the animosity between North and South – that is between the Northern Free States and the Southern Slave States. This war was evident in the newspapers. It reminded me strongly of the Irish and English newspapers.

Nearly every Northern newspaper that I saw outraged the feelings of the people of the South. Needless to say the Southern newspapers were not slow to pay back blow for blow. It was a strange state of affairs.

In the confederacy of states known as the United States of America slavery was a recognised institution. But according to many of the Northern newspapers the people of the slave states were all criminals of the worst kind. But slavery had not been introduced into the states by the people of the South.[1]

I believe it was begun by the New Englanders under the authority of the English Governors. I believe it continued to exist in the Northern states until it became unprofitable and unnecessary owing to the extensive immigration from Europe. I believe it is not recorded that the Northern owners of slaves, even under these circumstances, gave them their freedom. Possibly a few may have done this.

But I believe it cannot be denied that the Northern owners of slaves, when they no longer required them for their own service sold them to the Southerners for the highest price they could get for them.[2]

And I believe it was after this that they became abolitionists!

As far as my observation enabled me to judge – the people of the South were not proud of the Institution. I head the matter discussed in

New Orleans – with a view to finding out how to end it. I believe that a reasonable plan might and ought to have been devised by the Congress, which would have been more patriotic as more philanthropic than the vitriolic diatribes in the newspapers which gradually but inevitably led to the terrible civil war.

A system of gradual manumission would also have been better for the slaves as well as for the great industries concerned. I think I had read Mrs Beecher Stowe's 'Uncle Tom's Cabin' before I went to America. But I saw so little of what that book describes that I consider it to have grossly exaggerated.

The Institution was to my mind indefensible and doubtless led to frightful abuses. But I should say it would be nearly as unjust to denounce the English as a nation of wife beaters as to describe the slave owners of the southern states lumped together as bad and as wicked as Mrs Beecher Stowe described them.

During the war it struck me forcibly that if there was even a substratum of truth in Mrs B. Stowe's book the slave owners would not have dared to go out and fight, leaving their homes and their families at the mercy of their slaves.

To a large extent I believe the constitution of things prevailing on the plantations and in the domestic circle generally was of the most genial and friendly character – almost patriarchal.

I have seen sales of slaves at auction room in New Orleans – very sad sights truly; and other sad and bad things also hung on to the Institution. But that was no reason why North and South might not have considered together as to the *best* way to end it – instead of making it an excuse for slaughtering each other and ending it in the *worst* way.

The unfortunate negroes suffered terribly from the sudden change. Hitherto they had no need to be troubled about tomorrow. And without any provision for their maintenance they were suddenly thrown upon their own resources. In my opinion it would be about equally wise to have released from parental control all white children of nine years old; supposing that there were none older to help or guide them. For I believe that the intellect of the average negro, as it presented itself to me, was about equal to that of the average child of nine years.[3]

The question of slavery was not the only one between North and South. The North was a manufacturing country while the South and West was almost entirely agricultural; and while the import duties on European goods required by those agriculturists varied, then I think from fifteen to thirty-five per cent, this was practically a tax paid by them for the benefit of the Northern manufacturers.

I thought when I saw the insulting language constantly indulged in by the newspapers that war was bound to come. One thing was very remarkable – there were none whom I had met more resolutely pro-Southern than men who had come from the New England states.

I remember when the vote was taken for and against secession. Everyone was amazed at the great majority in favour of secession. There was great enthusiasm in New Orleans on that occasion. Immediately regiments of volunteer militia were enrolled for city defence.

In the 3rd district in which I then lived, a regiment was formed composed of married men. It was largely if not entirely Irish and this regiment I joined. When it was known by the leading men of the regiment that I had been a medical student for some years, I was selected for the post of Assistant Surgeon. My commission as such turned up on my trial for High Treason in 1867.

I think that the devotion to their cause exhibited by the Southerners has not often been surpassed in the historical records of struggles of the kind.

Of course many people of wealth were considerably interested in the Institution of slavery. But these did not constitute the majority nor a large proportion of the populations of the cities and towns.

Yet these voted for secession enthusiastically. Young men holding good situations as clerks, accountants, bookkeepers, in the stores and offices – left their snug berths in numbers, accepting the ordinary pay of the private soldier – $13 per month. Their usual salaries varied from $75 to $200 per month.

The leading ladies of New Orleans formed themselves into an association for preparing all kinds of necessaries for the soldiers. And at this they worked increasingly. There had existed a body of volunteer artillery – who used to parade on great public festivals. It was called the Washington Artillery. It was composed of wealthy young men.

Whenever they went out for drill or practice everyone of them – privates as well as officers – brought a man servant.

The Corps was yet a portion of the volunteer militia of Louisiana. But after a time when they volunteered for service in the field I suppose they then became a portion of the regular Army of the Confederate States, and of course had to conform to the regular discipline.

One of the first regiments that left New Orleans was largely Irish. The senior captain was named Nolan. I remember his appearance. He was about 5ft 10in, sandy complexion, yellowish moustache and chin beards, cheek bones rather prominent, well built, no superfluous flesh.

I think he was a member of the St Vincent de Paul Society, to which I also belonged. He was also president of the New Orleans branch of the Fenian Organisation – to which of course I also belonged. This branch was formed on the occasion of a visit by James Stephens in 1858. This was the first time I had met Stephens. Of course I intend to refer to him later.

This regiment of volunteers from New Orleans took part in the Battle of Bull Run – if my recollection be not at fault. It certainly very early went into action with the result that, all his superior officers having lost their lives, Nolan was colonel of the regiment after the battle.

Another regiment which left New Orleans and took part in the battle of Bulls Run was known as the Louisiana Tigers.[4] I remember what a spectacle these men made the day they marched out of the city. There was no pretense of uniformity in dress or equipment. They were mostly ill dressed, every man in his ordinary garb, with this addition: each carried an overcoat or a blanket rolled up and strapped on to some sort of knapsack – or made into a kind of ring and slung over the left shoulder.

These men were said to have been the corner boys of the city – a loose lot surely. But as to their fighting qualities, these were well proved at Bull Run.[5] They left New Orleans with such firearms as they could get – all sorts. A few had bayonets fixed to rifles. Some had long knives tied on to their guns. Some carried bowie knives. Some again bid knives (not so large as machettes [*sic*] used in Nicaragua for hewing away the brush wood) which had been hammered out of black iron and hung naked by the side.

But after Bull Run, these men left the field armed with the best rifles of the Northern soldiers.

The Tigers left their Commander-General Wheat dead on the field. He was I believe my acquaintance of Nicaragua or his brother.

Many of the LA Tigers were Irish. Many of the men, who left New Orleans for war, left behind them relatives of whom they were the chief support. And the resources of these people quickly failing, the municipal authorities and the community in general promptly organised a system of relief for them.

Money was voted by the municipality for this purpose. Contributions came in from all sides in money or materials. Wheat, corn, flour, meal, casks of pork and bacon, butter, articles for war. Commodities of all kinds were constantly arriving from the town along the river and from the plantations. The leading citizens formed a great committee for the distribution of these goods to the relatives of the soldiers.

The distribution was made by a certain number of leading men taking the work in rotation. The distribution was made twice a week – and it was called the free market. In addition to the bacon and pork above mentioned, fresh meat also was received and distributed.

From the beginning of the war times soon began to get hard for all persons whose income depended on their employment. For trade came to a stop. All kinds of local securities, property of every description – houses, lands etc – became of little or no value. Rents were rarely paid except by the strong and wealthy, especially those having business connections outside.

The ordinary currency, gold, silver and banknotes, disappeared. The only money in circulation were the bonds and notes of the Confederate government. These of course were made legal tender. And many to whom debts were due preferred to take change for payments in the future rather than accept this currency.

There were of course in the city many who were not in sympathy with the South in the war and these would decline to accept payment in Confederate notes. But this was soon found to be unsafe. Scarcely any one would run the risk of what might happen if it were made known that he had refused to accept payment of a debt in Confederate notes.

Doubtless, unfair advantage was taken of the state of things. For those able to command exchange with the outside world were able to buy Confederate notes and bonds at very heavy discount, until finally on the surrender of the city to Admiral Farragut and the notes of the Confederacy were worth only 8 cents per dollar, and when General Ben Butler took possession the Confederate currency no longer circulated in New Orleans.[6]

An old friend to whom I had lent some money repaid me when every dollar of the money he gave me represented in value but eight cents of the money I had lent him. I did not grumble, but I would have preferred he had remained in my debt with the knowledge that he would never be able to pay me – for I had received kindnesses from him.

For a fortnight while the city was beset by the Federal War Ships, provisions of all kinds except Indian meal could not be had. I think the Federals had cut off supplies from above as well as below.

During that time my family in common with many others fared badly. Indian meal being one chief article of diet – but we managed to buy a ham and some potatoes from the relatives of soldiers. This supply was maintained to the last, but probably it was stopped by General Butler.

When in the beginning of the war silver coin disappeared there was of course great difficulty in carrying on the every day trading – for there was small money required in the settlement of purchases. This difficulty was soon met by the issue of small notes by the important business houses. Notes for all sums from 5 cents to $2.50 were given as change at the large shops and stores – these were called by the not very euphonious name of Shin Plasters.

When General Butler took possession of the city he immediately issued an order that these Shin Plasters should be redeemed within thirty days on penalty of confiscation of the property of those by whom issued. At this time business was at a stand still in New Orleans – there stores were all closed. Shops, especially important ones, were called stores.

There was a certain establishment in the manufactured leather trade – harnesses, etc – whose book-keeper went out to carry on similar business for the Confederate Army and I was invited to wind up the accounts of the Firm. The Shin Plasters issued by this house in the various small sum necessary for 'making change' in the settlement of accounts amounted to about $30,000.

It happened that a gentleman who was a friend to the members of this firm was also acquainted with Colonel Andrew Butler, brother of General Butler, and through this gentleman an arrangement was brought about – for an advance of $30,000 to enable them to redeem their shin plaster. Col. Butler, who I believe in the matter represented General Butler was to receive $2,000 for the use of the money for one month.

But in working out the arrangement when $5,000 was advanced a draft was given to Col. Butler, payable on demand (I think), for such round sum of $5,000 or $6,000 on the Philadelphia firm of which this New Orleans house was an off-shoot. And when all the shin plasters had been redeemed I prepared a statement showing what proportion of the $2,000 was due to Colonel Butler, on the basis of a loan of $30,000 for a month. I found that but about one-fourth of the $2,000 was due to Butler. Butler, however, was master in New Orleans, thus his will was the law from which there was no appeal. And he sent word that unless the $2,000 was paid at once he would foreclose the mortgage – which he got from them off all their property as security for his loan. Of course the money was paid without further demand.

The trade of the city was at this time entirely killed off. There was no longer cotton, sugar, tobacco, corn – the chief products which found an outlet at New Orleans – coming down the river. The cotton was diverted to those ports which were in the hands of the Confederates, whence as much as possible was run through the blockade.

The other goods were sent to the Confederate Army and to the towns which were loyal to the Confederacy. What fortunes were made in cotton that succeeded in escaping the blockade! It was bought at eight cents a pound *in Confederate Currency* and in Liverpool it was worth a very high price then. Many ships and cargoes were captured but *not* a few ran the blockade successfully.

Some time before Federal ships of war came up to the city – and when the mouth of the Mississippi was blockaded by some five or six large ships some ingenious person or persons conceived the idea of preparing a new sort of engine. This consisted of the hull of a small but very strongly built vessel. The deck was rounded and together with the sides all was covered with railway iron firmly fastened on.

In the fore part was an opening in which was placed a good sized canon. A strong ram was fixed to the prow. I think this vessel had been a tug boat. It was provided with steam. This engine was named the 'Guyascutus'. It was filled up at Algiers – a suburb of New Orleans at the other side of the river.

Everyone went to see it, for naturally it excited great interest and curiousity. The general impression was that it was a crazy idea and not one in a thousand believed it could accomplish anything like what the inventors and promoters expected. For the invention was to raise the blockage of the mouth of the river by attacking the Federal ships.

In due time the vessel started on her mission – I believe it was the first iron clad vessel put afloat – in charge of an undoubtedly brave and daring crew. And in a few days New Orleans was astounded and delighted with the news: that the 'Cumberland' (this was I think the name of the largest of Federal war ships on the blockade of the river) had been disabled by the 'Guyascutus' and that the other ships in endeavouring to avoid the unknown monster had suffered damage in various ways. How much of this news was true I never afterward learned.

A few words as to why no fight was made for the defence of New Orleans. After the exploit of the 'Guyascutus' – which there were no means of following up – the blockade of the mouth of the Mississippi was soon reestablished. And rumours came that we might soon expect Admiral Faragut with some of the new Federal iron-clads.

For a time there was talk of putting up batteries at the place where the British were defeated in the War of 1812. But it was soon obvious that – the river level being then high, a ship on the river could easily command any battery on the land. Why no floating batteries were not constructed is I believe that the material for such could not be procured.[7]

The river was therefore undefended. And when Farragut was ready he had but to steam up the river, and with his big ships – heavily armed, lying opposite the city – his guns some 50 feet higher than the level of the city, New Orleans was at his mercy.

Under all the ups and downs I had passed through I had been able to save but a small sum. I was well able to calculate how long I could remain waiting for the revival of trade. But how long I should have to wait for this revival, I was unable to calculate.

Then having a wife and two children depending on me – a stepson and my own son – I concluded that I would return to Ireland. I found that after defraying expenses of passage to New York and thence to Queenstown I should [line missing].

During the war and up to the entrance of the Federal troops into New Orleans the Governor of Louisiana had his headquarters in a house belonging to the party for whom I had been doing business. General Butler on coming to the city took up possession of the same house for his headquarters.

There was then owing to me about $350 – by the owner of that house, while the only currency in peoples hands was that of the Confederate States with General Butler had banned and forbidden.

It was under my circumstances most desirable that while I had the means of transporting myself and family to Ireland, I should act promptly. This $350 was a large item in my assets but how could it be converted into current coin? After turning the matter over anxiously I decided on a step which appeared worth trying at all events.

My view was that General Butler by taking possession of the house recently vacated by the Governor of Louisiana had stepped into his shoes as tenant of the house. And I said to the owner of the house, 'I want to leave for Ireland; Confederate notes would therefore be useless to me, and as you have at present no other money – give me an order on General Butler for the sum due to me as part payment of the rent due to you.'

Of course I was by no means confident, indeed I was not even very hopeful as to the result of this move.

However, I got the order on General Butler and I sent it to him with a letter. After a few days I received an order for the amount payable, at some bank I think, not in gold but in greenbacks – United States notes, which I converted into gold at about 30 per cent discount.

I now lost no time in making the necessary preparations for departure. I found a ship about to sail for New York and I arranged for the sale of my furniture.

Then I found that no one was allowed to leave without a 'Pass' from General Butler. Having learned where application should be made I called at the time indicated and having handed in a letter explaining my destination and the number of my family, after a while I was brought before the General.

This was the first and only occasion when I saw him face to face. He was probably between 45 and 50 years old, complexion very fair, hair and beard light yellow, face rather short, broad in the upper part, jaws also square, height about 5ft 8in, one shoulder distinctly higher than the other. He spoke to me for a minute or so – and then pointed to the room where I would receive the desired 'pass.'

Before taking final leave of the General I will repeat here a story that was current. One never knew what to believe during the war. The newspapers were glad to get hold of any sort of rumour that would fit in with the probabilities. If circumstances required that it should be contradicted in a day or two – why that was so much new copy. But this style of thing is not unusual, even in the piping times of peace with the biggest journals in the biggest of cities (London).

A body of troops under Butler's command marched out from the city and went through the state of Louisiana. The story is that wherever they went they treated the people barbarously, that they broke down the bank or levée confining the waters of Lake Pontchartraine thereby causing the inundations of the neighbouring country to the extent of 500 miles (whether square miles or lineal I do not know).

It was also stated and believed that Col. Andew Butler had been heard boasting that on their return to New Orleans – that they swept the country bare – carrying away with them whatever was portable and burning what they could not carry.

This it was I suppose that gave rise to the epithet 'Spoons' which for years after was coupled with Benjamin Butler's name especially in Northern Newspapers – referring of course to the silver ware said to have been carried away from private houses on that occasion.

The state of feeling towards the Federal troops on the part of the citizens, the ladies especially, up to the time of my departure was exceedingly bitter.

New Orleans is not far from the tropics and the people of warm latitudes are naturally much warmer in their feelings and temperaments than those in higher latitudes; this is recognised all the world over, and accordingly is taken with consideration when judging their actions.

For a week or two after the Federals had taken possession of New Orleans it was like a city of the dead. Shops and stores of all kinds closed, private houses with persiennes closed. No one on the streets but the Federal soldiers in their simple uniform of dark blue cloth.

The young men had long since gone out as volunteers. The volunteer militia enrolled for protection of the city which remained largely composed of married men, and even of these, many regiments, when the surrender of the city became inevitable, held meetings and on vote being taken agreed to go out and join the Confederate army.

A meeting of the regiment to which I was attached was held to consider this question and the distinct majority voted against going out.

A few weeks after General Butler had resumed command of the city he sent around officers to the various business establishments with instruction more or less peremptory that the places of business should be reopened. And these were gradually complied with.

The people also walked about the streets. The ladies, the more strong minded ladies among them. These latter soon had frequent encounters with Federal officers.

I have no doubt that many officers, out of consideration for the humiliation of the citizens, took no notice of the provoking language of the ladies. Some of them however resented it and had several ladies arrested – it was even said that a few ladies had been flogged. But many stories circulated that were not quite true.

When remarking that people so near the tropics have warmer feelings than those living in higher altitudes I ought to have mentioned an instance of the effect of climate which came under my own eyes. I met in New Orleans a family which had formerly lived with my grand-father Matthew O'Brien, farmer. They brought with them some of their children born in Ireland and they had one daughter born in New Orleans. The father and mother and the children born in Ireland accus-tomed to work were of the ordinary Irish labourer class and style in features and general build, rather coarse featured, strong limbed, generally rough looking. While the daughter born in New Orleans was quite different. Her features were on finer lines, complexion not so clear a white and none of the red to be seen in the faces of the others, her limbs were also much more graceful. No one would have thought that she was of the same family.

I left New Orleans 22 October 1862 with my wife and two children, one of them my stepson, on board a sailing ship bound for New York. There was no vessel offering for Liverpool or any part of Europe. The ship was laden with cotton and sugar. I had no idea how unpleasant and disagreeable a cargo of sugar can make a ship. The stench becomes very bad in a few days. The gilding and the white paint were much tarnished from the fumes of the sugar.

Happily the weather was fine and warm so that we remained on deck day and night without inconvenience, with pleasure rather. I cannot recall any incident in connection with that voyage to New York. But when we got into the harbour the ship was boarded by a gang of men of whom the captain, and his chief officers, the whole crew indeed, were evidently in mortal terror.

They swarmed over the ship and down into the forecastle. The captain nor any other dared to not say them, nay, and in a short time they carried off with them a large number of the crew, bag and baggage.

These men were boarding house runners or touts – and they carried off the men to sailors' boarding houses – where, I believe there is not reason to doubt – every penny of the wages due to them would be spent in riotous living. And in addition an advance on account obtained from the next ship they would engage for.

I cannot conceive a system more terrible. Why it is tolerated I cannot imagine.

I spent about five days in New York and during that time I had the pleasure of making the acquaintance of John O'Mahony.

He was I believe a self-sacrificing and devoted patriot. His height must have been near 6 ft. He was of light build, his face was long and narrow, good regular features, complexion pale, no colour in his face, hair dark and rather long. He was more of the style of the student than the man of action. I felt attracted to him, but did not have much opportunity of meeting him.

I did not see much of New York. I can remember only the Bowery, Madison Square, the Park (then quite new), and the new Catholic Cathedral (the walls of which were then about ten feet high). We took the first steamer for Queenstown where we landed in due course, and went on to Cork without delay.

Chapter 6

At Home Organising, 1862–1867

I at once set about finding employment and after a few weeks was successful. I was engaged as book-keeper by Messrs James Clery and Co, wholesale tea and wine merchants.[1] I was General Manager as well as book-keeper. I attended so well to my work and gave so much satisfaction that when the 6th March 1867 came around my remuneration was about three times as much as the salary at which I engaged in December 1862.

[The following short section is written in Alfred Webb's hand, presumably from previous drafts.]

Way now opened for carrying out the main object of my life – the devotion to an attempt to shake off the tyranny of England and assert the nationality of my country. All my life had led up to it. I imbibed my [illegible] from no one. They must have come from that god who made me – for they were in my heart and in my blood from my earliest years.

I have already told how my young blood thrilled as I read the Battle of Ventry Harbour, how my heart was filled with the longing that I might even, as the boys of [illegible] in that narration, fight for Ireland. As I passed from childhood into boyhood and read that terrible narrative of fraud and oppression – the history of Ireland – the more was my heart filled with hatred of the oppressor. How I sympathised with the Repeal and Young Ireland movement which went down in the abyss of the Famine and the misfortunes of 1848.

In 1849, as I have told, I joined a movement which had but a brief existence and came to a fruitless end in the attack on the police barrack at Cappoquin. For my complicity in this affair I had for a time to leave Ireland. Then came my student days, and my foreign adventures. All through, as had been seen, I kept myself closely in touch with those who had suffered for or were still strong for Ireland.

Before I met James Stephens in New Orleans in 1858, I had joined the Irish Republican, or more commonly known as the Fenian Brotherhood, for the liberation of Ireland.[2]

I do not feel that any excuse is necessary for the part I took in this organisation. There was ample reason for the feeling that found part of my nature. Apart from the centuries of [illegible] of my religion and oppression of my country that lay behind, but thirty years before my birth the free legislature of Ireland had been broken down by fraud and force. Any sort of religious equality had been worked as long as possible. The Established Church of the minority stood – draining its principal revenues from a poor people of a different faith.[3] (In the district where I was born it was not more than 5% of the population was Protestant).[4] I had seen a moral force effort for the [illegible] of our legislative rights broken down by the government. I had seen a Famine such as had in recent ages never before devastated a civilized country pass over my land. I had seen food in plenty exported, whilst the population starved. I had seen what had never before in a time of peace and within a similar period occurred in history, the population reduced by one third. The bottom of the [illegible] was strewed with the remains of those who perished of disease and hardship in the foul vessels into which they crowded in the necessity of getting away – anywhere – anywhere from their native land and from under the British flag. Worse than all I had seen in the great American cities the degradation brought upon the thousands of as pure and high a womanhood as ever breathed, the [illegible] ignorant help- less – many of them speaking a different language – upon a foreign shore.

The [illegible] cause of most of these accumulated miseries was the maintenance of an [illegible] Land System which had on a government [illegible] been full exposed before the Famine; to all [illegible] of which an alien governments turned a deaf ear, maintaining it as necessary for a continuance of the cold hearted policy through which it upheld its ascendancy.

The people of any other country in the world would under like conditions have felt and acted as we did. The chances of success of the movement were our [illegible]. The conditions were different from what they are now. Modern [illegible] military weapons had not been invented. The relative population of Ireland was greater. Thousands of her sons, eager and anxious to grow any such enterprise, had been fully blamed in the use of arms in one of the greatest conflicts of the century.

In any case we were found in [illegible] to make the attempt. Peace to the many noble souls now no more, with whom a common purpose brought me into communion. Many who [illegible] are my best friends. Their character and intentions have been fully [illegible].

[End of the part in Webb's handwriting.]

I do not remember how I got in touch with the IRB in Cork – possibly it was through John O'Leary. I have no doubt that I must have written him or met him somewhere some time after I had settled down. At all events in the course of a year or so I got to know some of the most active of them – Bryan Dillon, John Kenneally, James Barrett, Michael Murphy, John J. Geary, Dominick O'Mahony.

Bryan Dillon was a solicitor's clerk. He was hunch-backed. Full of enthusiasm, ready to do and dare anything for Ireland's sake. He had the artists' temperament, of which I think there is a large share among the young men of Cork. He was full of the desire and ambition to distinguish himself in connection with the movement of the Organisation – Dillon, Kenneally, and Barrett were chums and were usually together in the evenings. The two latter were assistants in the dry goods establishments known as the Queen's Old Castle Co.[5] Sober mannered, but entirely devoted to the cause. Dillon had the most active mind; the others rather followed his initiative. Dillon's physique was rather fragile, the other two were strong men, Barrett I believe was something of an athlete. Kenneally was the only one of the three now living. As least when last heard of – a few years ago – he was a prosperous man at Los Angeles, California.

Poor Geary cleared out in 1865 – and met a terrible death in some American town – Cincinnati I think – by falling into a vessel of boiling oil or some such matter. Michael Murphy was a hatter and had a shop in Great Georges Street. Dominick O'Mahony – I am not sure what he was – he was certainly naturally an orator. The poor man was addicted to drink and I fear this is still his case.

I undertook to give rudimentary lessons in drill to a few men in my own house. I then lived in a small house in a little square, on the North Mall.

The most notable event in this year which I can recollect was the starting of the *Irish People* newspaper with John O'Leary as editor. He sent me a copy of the first number. It was, I think, in this year I first met O'Donovan Rossa.

Word had gone out that James Stephens was to meet the leading men of the county at the house of John J. Geary. The way this was talked about amazed me – it appeared to me simply impossible that the police could be so ignorant of what was on the topics – for it was talked among every group of men wherever gathered.

I had occasionally to meet some of the men I have mentioned at public houses – they sometimes called at my house but the public houses were the usual rendez-vous. Then I was shocked to observe how recklessly the IRB men talked of the affairs of the Organisation. There was no pretence of reticence unless indeed a policeman *in uniform* was present. It was obvious to me that to know all that was going on, the policemen had only to exchange his uniform for the ordinary dress of a working man or artisan, and go around the public houses. I called attention to this state of affairs but to no purpose.

But on the occasion of Stephens's visit to Cork, the day before and the day or two he remained, the northern end of the North Main Street, in which Geary's public house was situated, was in a manner openly patrolled by numbers of the leading men who had come in from outlying parts of the country.

I should say that this visit of Stephens's to Cork was little short of notorious. And yet we were engaged in a conspiracy respecting which *secrecy* was vitally important. I suppose at least three hundred men met Stephens on this occasion – these hundreds were constantly going into and out of the house, a crowd of them in the shop standing about and talking.

Rossa had just got married to his third wife, a Miss Irwin of Clonakilty, and on the day of the marriage, I think, came to this gathering bringing the bride with him.[6]

He had arranged with Geary that they were to have a room in Geary's house, for himself and wife, but the room was given up to Stephens, and when coming away about 11 p.m., I heard Rossa grumbling and lamenting that now at this hour he did not know where to look for accommodation.

This was the first time I had met Rossa, but the case appeared to me to be a hard one for the young wife, and I decided on straining a point (for in my little abode we had but barely sufficient room for our little family). However, I offered Rossa accommodation for the night, which of course he gladly accepted.

I was not at all satisfied with what I saw of the working of the Organisation. I asked some questions as to what provision was being made for arming the people. I say *people* advisably, for without any doubt the vast bulk of the people were heart and soul with the conspiracy. Yes, the people, whose hearts are always and always will be full of devotion to Ireland, always ready to lay down their lives for her – had entirely recovered from the awful Famine and the depressing disappointment of 1848 and 49, were breast high for revolution, meaning a fight for Ireland's freedom.

In reply to my questions I was told that Stephens had undertaken the charge of providing everything necessary, and that depots of arms were being prepared in various places and there were rumours of vessels landing arms from America. However I wrote to John O'Leary suggesting that it could do no harm if the men were encouraged to provide arms for themselves. After a while I received a reply to the effect that – he had spoken with Stephens on the subject, that he (Stephens) would not consent to the men providing arms for themselves, but that Stephens would provide them.

I was only nominally a member of the organisation, was practically a stranger in Cork, and meeting at rare intervals only the three men Dillon, Kenneally and Barrett – there was a fourth man who was also of this lot and one of the chums. He was also an assistant in a dry good house, possibly the same house – his name was O'Shaughnessy. I cannot now remember what became of him, whether he went away or died. I think he died – and I think it was after that that Barrett in a manner filled his place, the vacancy thus created. These were the leading men of the IRB Cork.

Murphy was one of the men I used to drill at my house – but he did not keep it long and after that I saw very little of him. O'Mahony I met and saw very rarely – except when he orated at a public meeting.

I think it must have been early in 1865 that Stephens next visited Cork. He apparently recognised the imprudence of the circumstances attending his previous visit – the publicity and the crowds – for on this occasion his visit was private and only a few people were brought to see him. I was one of those so honoured. Mrs Stephens accompanied her husband.

On each of these two visits a great amount of homage was paid to Stephens – even the leading men of the county did not presume to have opinions of their own – no one hesitated to accept Stephens's word for law. No one ventured to ask for explanations. My position in the Organisation did not entitle me to be present at those interview with Stephens. It was a kind of special favour. In Ireland James Stephens was at the time I write of more completely a political autocrat than the Russian Czar. Not even the leading men on the staff of the *Irish People* newspaper – O'Leary, Luby and Kickham, who acted as a sort advising Councillors – presumed to have opinions of their own in opposition to those of Stephens – or to question the soundness of his views.

When in 1868 I joined Luby and O'Leary at Portland Prison where we three worked within a few feet of each other, I learned from Luby in the presence of O'Leary that Stephens had taught them to accept him as a genius without compeer – that it chose to set himself to the work he could surpass the greatest men such as Raphael, Michael Angelo, Shakespeare, etc. One of his great ideas was to build a great city at Kilkenny on in that neighbourhood in a style of architecture which would harmonise with the scenery of the place.

Luby said that while ashamed of the influence Stephens had exercised over them he was afraid that if they were released and circumstances brought them together again, Stephens would soon regain his ascendancy over their minds.

The impression left upon my mind was that O'Leary accept [*sic*] this as a correct statement. If he dissented at all it was very mildly.

It is right to say here that some years later when I met Kickham – while confirming Luby's statement as far as Luby and O'Leary were concerned he was not himself dominated by Stephens as they were. Certainly there was nothing to restrain Stephens's hands – he was complete master in Ireland. In his case One Man Power had a free hand.

In two other very remarkable men it had practically an equal free hand. I refer to O'Connell and Parnell.[7]

In the ranks of the Irish Parliamentary Party there is now a feeling that the system of government by Chairman plus Committee has failed. I may return to this later – in due course.

I had met Stephens three times: first at New Orleans about 1858, secondly and thirdly at Cork as I have described a few pages earlier, and I am bound to say I cannot understand how he had succeeded in imposing himself on O'Leary and Luby, each of whom in my opinion was decidedly his superior intellectually.

Stephens never impressed me particularly. I saw how he ruled others and subjugated their minds and I thought, 'I suppose there must be more in the man than I am able to discern,' and I was quite ready to be convinced by experience. But my belief is he never was the man he was believed to be.

I think it was after the Stephens gathering of 1864 that I went on a little tour with Rossa to Dungarvan and other places in the County Waterford for the purpose of strengthening the Organisation there.

After that I did not see Rossa for many years – though we were in the same prison, Millbank London about 1868.

I return to Stephens's visit to Cork in 1865. He put up at a private house in the Lower Glanmire Road. For the purpose of mentioning that, when I had returned home that night I found I had left a cane at the house – and I called for it the next day.

This visit of Stephens though so private, appears to have attracted more notice from the police than his previous visit as I found later.

I think it was in September 1865 that the Government counter-plot had ripened, the police made a raid on the premises of the *Irish People* newspaper, swept off all the papers from the desks, drawers and files in the offices and a large quantity of printed material – arrested O'Leary, Luby, Rossa, James O'Connor and many others in Dublin.[8] About the same time all the leading men in Cork and elsewhere were carried off to prison – among them Bryan Dillon, Kenneally and O'Shaughnessy.

After a day or two I went to Dublin to make an offer of my services if I could be useful in any way. I called on Joe Dennieff, merchant tailor, South Ann Street and he invited me to stop at his house. I found that he was in almost daily communication with Stephens – who was living very privately in the suburbs. Kickham was with him.

The medium was a young lady about 14 years old. I omit her name lest she may not like to have it mentioned. Indeed I do not know whether she is living now.

At Dennieff's house I met a number of men who were engaged in the work of the IRB – General D. F. Burke, General Millen and others. Millen did not impress me favourably.

When I found that I could not be of any use in Dublin, I thought I would venture on a visit to John Martin. The place was named Loughshore (I think). It was situated beautifully at the foot of the Moran Mountains[9] and looking down upon Carlingford Lough. This had been the residence of his brother who had died not long before this time, and John Martin was guardian of his brother's children.

I enjoyed very much my visit of a few days in this delightful place. Martin had nothing to do with the IRB. I think he rather disapproved of it.

Not long after my return to Cork – I was absent little more than a week – I had a visit at the offices of Messrs Clery and Co from two gentlemen whom I did not know. They said they wished to speak to me in private – and I took them to a private office. We had scarcely seated ourselves when one of the gentlemen, by way of introduction, said I am Mr ——— Resident Magistrate and this is Mr ——— Inspector of Police (I cannot now reveal the names of those gentlemen). Up to this I was under the impression that the visitors had called on business connected with the establishment of which I was manager. I rather think it was hoped that this brusque announcement would agitate me and throw me off my balance.

It so they were entirely disappointed – for I did not show the slightest sign of uneasiness. I made no reply, but merely bowed slightly in acknowledgement of the introduction. The RM went to say they called about my visit to James Stephens on a day (which they mentioned) at a certain house (which they named) on the Lower Glanmire Road. To show me that their information was accurate and that I could not deny the visit – they told me that I called back to the house the next day for my cane, which I had left there, forgotten to take away with me.

After reciting this the RM began to ask me questions – whether I had visited Stephens, whom I saw there, etc. To which I replied, 'You have told me that you know everything about this already. Why then do you ask me questions?' Having pressed me as to whether I had visited Stephens, I did not care to make any bother about it and I said yes I had met Mr Stephens in America some years ago and I was glad to take the opportunity for seeing him. The RM now appeared to think he had made an impression upon me and he wanted to know whom I saw with Stephens. I declined to give him any information. He then began a homily on my duties as a loyal citizen and the allegiance I owed to her majesty the Queen. Here I cut him rather short, telling him how he was quite mistaken – that I owed no allegiance to the Queen of England, for I was an American citizen.

My two gentlemen were now completely dumbfounded. I stood on my American citizenship and they could only grumble, 'That accounts for things!' And they left me.

Soon after they had gone Mr Clery Senior came to me in a state of alarm, expressing fervently the hope that they had nothing against me. The old gentleman was a J.P. for the country – his son Mr John W. Clery, who was now carrying on the business, as a J.P. for the city – and both of them as became men of large means were most loyal citizens, having of course not the slightest sympathy with the IRB movement. However I believe I had won the respect and good will of both of them. I had certainly devoted myself to the business and with considerable success for in less than three years my remuneration had been trebled.

Mr John W. Clery was also distressed about my visitors. As far as I could judge both the Messrs Clery were aware that the visit was in contemplation. I suppose the matter was discussed at a meeting of the magistrates, for some days later the old gentleman congratulated me very heartily that they had nothing against me.

I had always been a most domestic man spending all my spare time with my family. Though I had been a few times at Geary's public house and a few other places for the purpose of meeting people, I was practically unknown, even to the police. I met the Police Inspector about four or five years later, at the Maryboro Railway Station, when he greeted me heartily. He had been promoted to RM. I have just called to mind his name: Hamilton.

After this for some months matters jogged along on the old groves as if nothing unusual had ever happened or was ever going to happen. But as in a volcanic region the natives can tell when and outburst is to be expected, so the underground political rumbling in Ireland was then perceptible to the initiated.

James Stephens's escape after some months from the Richmond Prison arrests in September '65 was traced to his hiding place, a respectable style of house in the suburbs where he lived as a private gentleman under the name of Herbert. A close watch was of course kept on all the well known men in and about Dublin and in course of time the one or two who were accustomed to carry messages from Stephens to some of those were gradually traced and, when the matters had ripened, a raid was made upon the house, and with James Stephens were also arrested Kickham and Ned Brophy. I am not sure of the Christian name.[10] I never had the pleasure of meeting Mr Brophy as far as I can recollect but I have many times heard of him with praise.

Stephens' arrest was a great shock to the IRB men. It reminds me now of the shock the country experienced when O'Connell was found guilty in 1844. For he was supposed to have entrenched him in an unassailable position. In like manner Stephens was, by the many credited with unequalled resources which would always place him beyond the reach of the enemy. And when the report of his arrest went abroad the masses received it with *resolute* incredulity. Which however had to give way very soon – causing great depression in the hearts of our people.

I forgot to mention that – while I was at Joe Dennieff's house he was almost daily expecting to see the police coming in to ransack the house and premises, and he spoke of a superior specimen of revolver which he had in the house which he should lose under such circumstances.

The morning that I was leaving I offered to take charge of the revolver and carry it wherever he wished – but he did not accept my offer. And I learned subsequently that within an hour of my having left the house the police were in the house and carried off himself and I think General D. J. Burke also. Had I remained I suppose I also would have been arrested then.

But if the arrest of Stephens depressed the hearts of the people, now am I to refer to his escape from Richmond Prison a few months after. His arrest was about the end of 1865 or the beginning of 1866, while his escape was I think about March '66.

The country was electrified by the first rumour: that Stephens escaped. It was almost taken off its feet delighted, intoxicated with joy. And not a doubt but that many a one did indeed get very really intoxicated indulging in a glass over the event. There was no longer depression in the ranks of the IRB men – their hopes and their confidence were higher than ever.

For now the belief was wide that Stephens permitted himself to be arrested that he might show the Government that the prison had not been built that could hold him.

But while the country was full of all kinds of versions of the story of the escape – all [illegible] to Stephens's fame – the anti-Irish Irishmen soon had their story too: that the Government had permitted Stephens to leave the prison and that he was now a tool of the Government – which of course was utterly false.[11]

The manner of the escape was clearly shown on the trial of the man who planned and affected it – Breslin – who was then in a position of trust in Richmond Prison – but fortunately it was not brought home to him with sufficient clearness to secure a conviction. And Breslin soon after went to America.

This reminds me of what Kickham told me respecting Stephens's escape – namely, that if Stephens had not been so nervously anxious about himself, Kickham also might have got away – then his cell being near that of Stephens. But considering Kickham's defects of sight and hearing it appears to me that the escape of Stephens would have been jeopardised had it been attempted to get off Kickham also.

Breslin, however, the hero of that great affair – and he deserves much credit for the manner in which he worked – single-handed I believe.[12]

The escape was a great relief to our friends whose spirits had been much depressed by the arrests. Their faith in Stephens was if possible greater than ever. Many were convinced that he suffered himself to be captured and imprisoned in order to show that no prison could hold him.

The suspense was however great for the desire was general that the rising should not be delayed. And those in the upper ranks of the Organisation were chafing and worrying, for two reasons in particular – It was believed that something like 8,000 of the soldiers in various garrison in Ireland had joined the Organisation, and there was great anxiety respecting them, lest they should become suspected and removed from Ireland before the rising, while of course many of them were every day in danger of arrest with its grave consequences.

There was also the case of the Irish American soldiers who had seen service in the great civil war. I think it was supposed that there were over 3,000 of them in Ireland waiting for the day. Everyday we were becoming more and more exposed to suspicion, and wasting resources.

As far as my observation enables me to form an opinion I should say that the only change of striking a blow with any prospect of was in 1865 or 1864, while the soldiers were ready to turn out, and would not have come empty handed, while there were also good hopes that they might be able to seize some depots of arms. Then also the Irish-Americans were ready, 'fresh, vehement and true.'[13]

As time passed, the suspected regiments were quickly sent out of Ireland, and several of those suspended men such as Sergeant Charles McCarthy (whom I met in Portland Prison), as fine, devoted, chivalrous, and self-sacrificing a patriot as I have ever met or care to meet – he and many others in like positions were arrested, tried, convicted and subjected to infamous treatment.

This splendid man's health was so shattered by ill treatment, that when he was released it was but to die in the arms of the friends in Dublin who had assembled in vast number to welcome him and others who had been released.

Other men besides the soldiers were then ready to join us – who became suspect – and their position made impossible.

By postponing the time for the rising it became impossible, childish in fact, much worse indeed on the part of the man who know the circumstances. Of course I mean Stephens. He got away to France and went thence to America.

As to what he did there my knowledge is very slight. As far as I gathered from various sources it would appear that his inaction and procrastinating were severely condemned by our friends here – that finally they became imperative and insisted that Stephens should fix for a day the rising. This was, as well as I recollect, after a great meeting in Jones's Wood – near New York I believe.

And, according as the matter has come to me, it would appear that Stephens left America for France about February of 1867 – about two or three weeks before 6th March in that year two ladies came to Cork: Miss O'Leary and Miss Duffy, sisters respectively of John O'Leary and Edward Duffy, both men closest in association and confidence with Stephens. I never met Edward Duffy though he died in Millbank Prison while I was there – about the end of 1867 or early in 1868: and I think that some stitching work given to me was poor Duffy's winding-sheet.

I heard a good deal of Ned Duffy before the rising. He was perhaps the most active of those connected with the province of Connacht. He was universally loved and trusted by those who knew him – and was one of Stephens's righthand men. I think he was arrested with Stephens and Kickham. He was engaged to Mary O'Leary – John's younger sister.

Stephens's letter was shown to me and others. We did not know the writing. The messengers, however, vouched for its authority. An effort was made to bring together the leading men of the IRB in the city. My position had not entitled me to be much considered in the workings of the movement in Cork. The leading positions had fallen in my mind to utterly incapable men.

I myself had nothing whatever to do with the working of the Organisation. I was a sort of un-attached member of it. I knew nothing of the people and was unable to be useful among them. So I gave all my time and attention to my business and my family.

Now, as early as 1864, I was not satisfied that adequate measures were being taken to provide arms. I wrote to John O'Leary who was then editor of the *Irish People* newspaper and well known to be in close relations with Stephens. I proposed that members of the Organisation ought be encouraged to provide themselves with arms. O'Leary replied that Stephens would not consent to this – but that he would take care to provide everything necessary. It was rumoured that depots of arms had been accumulated at various points; Mallow and Limerick Junction among others.

I do not remember whether there was any reference to those depots in that letter from Stephens – but when the question to be decided was: a *rising*, I strongly opposed it, for I did not believe in the depots, and I could not think of such as thing as a rising of unarmed men.

The questions was however carried against me – two of the men voting for the rising and whose votes decided the question did not join in the rising; one of them is dead – God be merciful to him! The other is I think still living.

Of course I felt bound in honour to see the matter out and to do my little best. I had been looking forward to this issue as a matter of course, and some 6 or 8 months earlier I had sold my furniture and removed my family to lodgings.

When the time was approaching I placed my children under the care of their grandmother and I took a room for myself on Warren's Place. And from this I took a cab to Prayer Hill on the night of the 5 March 1867.

I pause for a moment to mention an incident which took place a few days earlier. I think on the Saturday before 5 March. I was invited to call at Neelan's Hotel, King Street, and there I met Miss Duffy – who introduced me to General Massey who was to command at Limerick Junction. Massey was short of money to defray expenses – I gave him £10, out of the little reserve I kept for myself after having made some provision for my children. He was a very fine working man, about 6 ft high and well-proportioned, curly black hair and grand black moustache. But – 'handsome is that handsome does' – and judged by this rule, Massey was no better than a poltroon.

I believe Massey's arrest took place that night near or at Limerick Junction. According to the reports of the time he fainted. He became an informer.

I can however say that Massey was not as bad as he might have been. He was produced on my trial, but he swore that he had never seen me.

In Cork the rising was utterly dislocated by the arrest a few days before, of the men who were to have commanded, some Irish-American officers.

The cab I took with me to Prayer Hill was employed in a raid endeavoured to hunt up one or two of those men who were supposed to have escaped the attentions of the police. They could not be found.

Chapter 7

On the Hill-Side, 1867

———————

At Prayer Hill on Blarney Road there were gathered some 1,500 men – I was told that two other bodies were leaving by other roads – and that the total number was about 5,000. I must say I was very doubtful as to the way the men would turn out when called on, and the experience of that might entirely dispel all doubts as regards the men. Indeed, so long as Ireland's rights are denied her, I am satisfied that the young men and the old men of our country will never be slow or backward in responding to the call of duty. In '67 the men were there ready and willing but the *leaders* were wanting.

It saddens me to think of that crowd on Prayer Hill, every moment expecting that some sort of leader would turn up. But we waited in vain.

I have already said that my position in the IRB did not entitle me to assist at the discussion as to whether Stephen's order to rise should be complied with. In fact, I was a mere unit in the Organisation. My acquaintances with the people of Cork was very slight and consequently I held no position in the IRB, so that, when I joined the rising, I was – except to a very few – an unknown volunteer.

After waiting for leaders, for the best part of an hour after I reached Prayer Hill, it was at length decided – by whom I did not know – that we should move towards Mallow. There was an idea among some of the men that there was a depot of arms thereabouts. The men straggled along the road – a mere rabble.

I did think that although we did have the experienced Irish American officers expected, that we nevertheless had among us some men who, from their positions in the IRB, would come to the front and lead in *some* fashion.

When about to start the armament was counted up and the equip-ment of this body – 1500 to 1800 men – was found to consist of:

2 shot guns
1 rifle
5 revolvers
18 pikes

When we had been perhaps an hour on the march, noticing that no one had come to the front, with a view to leadership of any kind, two men were pointed out to me – who, it was supposed, had seen some service in America: Michael O'Brien (one of the 'noble hearted three' hanged at Manchester the next year) and Captain Mackey.[1]

I spoke to each of them – calling attention to the deplorably organ-ised condition of the party – and I suggested to them that they ought to take charge. Each of them declined. After an interval of half an hour or so, having considered the matter I said to them that – with their approval, I myself would take charge of such of the men as might be willing to fall in under my direction. They approved of this, and, having explained my desire to the men near me, the word passed around – and in a few minutes, some hundreds were marching in fours. To help them to keep step I get a few men at intervals in the ranks to whistles or sing marching tunes. Even this little effort I observed with satisfaction had an excellent effect on the men.

An incident which is perhaps worth noting took place previous to my intervention just described. About 6am we passed through a small village – 'Shovel-Mills' I think it was called. Our poor fellows were naturally hungry having spent the night in the sharp, cold air of that cold March night, and seeing a little shop in which was a supply of bread I suppose that, under the circumstances, nothing could be more natural than that they thought they had a right to requisition that bread. Indeed if it had been the shop of any other than a poor person I don't think there could have been any reasonable objection. It was, however, the shop of a poor person and considering how the raiding of this shop could be made to use of to our discredit, when I saw some of the men go towards this shop and I was able to gather that they had no intention of paying for the bread – as no one else took any notice, I ventured to act. Going to the door of the shop I called out aloud, 'Anyone who desires to take anything from this shop must pay for it, if he can, and I will pay for those who can't.' We therefore paid the poor woman for what was taken from her.

Of course a revolution could not be made on these terms. But, from the first, I had little doubt that we were conducting one of the most forlorn of forlorn hopes. I could not however say whether a depot of arms might not turn up somewhere. I did not in the least expect it, but, bearing in mind Stephens's undertaking, as conveyed to me by John O'Leary by letter, as already mentioned, it was *possible* that something of the kind had been done. Mallow had been talked of among the men as a place for such a depot of arms, and as we should be able to test this within some hours. And if the depot turned up we should be in a position to start the revolution, when we should of course requisition in some regular way the necessary supplies. While if there was no depot – as I felt certain would prove to be the case – we could do nothing but disband at once.

I do not mean to say – I reasoned out the case in this manner – in the minute or so within which I decided what to do at the little shop – I simply felt that it would be a shameful thing for us to deprive of her little stock this poor women who could not afford such a loss; and our enemies would be sure to use it for all it was worth to our discredit. I felt also that the course of that day would decide whether we should be an insurgent force or not. And if *not* it would be well to be self-supporting for that day as far as possible.

Resuming now my place on the line of march, where I broke off to describe the incident at 'Shovel-Mills' village, I remember that a house was visited on the way and one or two following piece were taken, for which acknowledgement was given. I forget the name of the person from whom taken – or by whom the receipt was signed.[2]

Between 8 and 10 o'clock in the morning we came to a place where a road to the left led on towards Ballynockin, some half mile off, where there was a police barrack.[3] A halt was called and after a consultation by a few who knew the district – it was decided that fifty men under Captain Mackey should go and attack the barrack. The intention was that the main body should wait were it was until Mackey and his party returned.

Under the circumstances I decided that I should go as a volunteer to Ballynockin. When we got about 200 yards from the barrack I observed one or two policemen on the road outside the house. As we advanced nearer they retired to the barrack and closed the door. It was rather a long, low, two-storied house with a frontage of 30 to 40 feet. The door was at the end by which we approached, as well as I could judge, the road we were upon led past the barrack on the Mallow. The house was some 12 places back from the road, the space between was fenced in by a low wall with an opening in the middle.

When we came up Mackey, having in his hand a rifle or shot gun, taken from one of the party, I think, for he had previously only a revolver, advanced to the door at which he knocked with the butt of his gun. There was no answer. He knocked again and in a loud voice he demanded the surrender of the policeman in the name of the Irish Republic. I think there was then an interchange of words between Mackey and the police. They refused to surrender.

Among the fifty who volunteered to come with Captain Mackey I now noticed some were mere boys, apparently about 15 years old. At his point – when the police refused to surrender – some of these boys with stones in their hands took up a position in front of the barrack and flung stones at the windows. I made them retire from such a position and take shelter of the wall which was in front of the house.

Mackey now endeavoured more than once to break in the door with the butt of his gun and again with a piece of wood, but his efforts were ineffectual. He exposed himself recklessly, I thought, taking up position in the middle of the space between the house and the road. However I felt it unbecoming to me that another should be more daring than myself, so notwithstanding that I thought it imprudent, I took my place by Mackey's side.

While in this position a shot from the barrack covered Mackey with the smoke of the powder. He turned half round to the right – I was on his left – apparently with the shock, but he did not stir from the spot. Of course I held my place beside him.

Before or after this I had been about the immediate neighbourhood and I saw a ladder laid against a house.

Mackey failing his efforts to get into the barrack proposed to give it up. But I said I should be ashamed to turn my back on such an affair. I told him were the ladder was and said, let us have that ladder and we will soon open the door. Instead of this Mackey got a piece of timber and with the help of one or two tried to break in the door – but the piece of timber was not sufficiently heavy. Again he came to me and proposed to give it up. I said, 'No, let us have the ladder.' Now not *my* ladder but a smaller one was brought up, and in the hands of four or five men, with one dash the door flew open. The police ran up the stairs. I proposed to rush after them, thinking that they were so scared they would not show fight. This suggestion was not acted upon. But the fire was taken from the grate of what was, I suppose, the orderly room and a fire was made under the stairs.

Possibly it was about this time that I learned that the Sergeant in charge of the barrack had a wife and children, and I desired that they should be sent out, which was done.

The progress of the fire under the stairs was sure but very slow. And the slowness was a source of imminent danger to us. We were but fifty – having an armament of three guns (a rifle and two shot guns) and two revolvers, Mackey's and mine. While the fire was under way I noticed a man on horse back come from a neighbouring house and ride quickly towards Mallow – only six miles off. I think he was a Mr [illegible]. I also observed walking up and down the road near the police barrack a priest who I learned was Father Neville, CC.[4]

The fire at length attacked the floor upon which the policemen had taken refuge, and after a while they appeared to think their position was becoming untenable for they asked that Father Neville might be called to speak with them. He came up and they asked him to advise them. He said, 'Well my men have you done your best?' They replied, 'We have sir.' He then said, 'If you do no more you are not bound to lose your lives.' This evidently satisfied them, for they now agreed to surrender –

the terms being that they should deliver of their arms before being allowed to descend the ladder, which was now placed at one of the upper windows from which the sash had been removed.

I stood at the foot of the ladder, my back to the road; the first policeman to descend, possibly not knowing or forgetting the terms, was carrying his rifle in his hand as he was stepping on to the ladder. I heard a few shots fired on the road to which my back was turned. I thought it was fired as *feu de joie*, rejoicing in the capture of the police barrack, but the policeman who was about to come down cried out that he had been fired at. I did not think this possible – and to appease what I thought groundless alarm, I desired the firing to be stopped. But it seems he had really good grounds for alarm, for I was told that the chin-strap of his cap had been cut by a bullet, close to his temple.[5]

After this incident the police handed down their rifles and then came down by the ladder. When our boys got the police rifles in their hands of course they handled them rather clumsily, with one slight mishap the result: a young fellow named Coughlan – a smart, intelligent man, of 25 years or so, got a bullet through his shoulder. Fortunately it was so high as to escape the lung. There was very little bleeding from it. I dressed the wound in some fashion on the spot. We now retired to Bottle Hill which was about half a mile from the barrack. Some of our peopled wished to take the police along as prisoners, but, to this I would not consent. Nor would I allow some of the policemen to join us, for I felt that we were not going to do any good. We were now close to Mallow and there was no word of the depot of arms, so I would not give the police greater opportunity than could be helped for identifying our fellows; nor would I allow them to ruin themselves by joining us under such circumstances. Of course I would have had their help with pleasure if there were any sign of our being in a position to make a decent stand.

At this stage of the business I heard myself addressed as Colonel O'Brien and it was one of the aliases in the indictment later on.

Having done our work at the Ballynockin Police Barracks we now moved on to Bottle Hill, where it was hoped we might learn something of the other bodies of men who had left Cork by other roads.

We had not rested more than 20 minutes when we saw advancing from the Mallow direction a body of infantry soldiers, about 80 or 100. Between Bottle Hill and the road was a large square field – with fences from four to six feet high. The soldiers came on through this field, which would have been a death trap for them if we had had a supply of arms and ammunition; but unarmed as we were we could do nothing but scatter. And this we did so thoroughly that at the end of two hours or so I found myself alone with a lad of 17 or 18 named Murphy who said he was apprenticed to a Coach-builder in Caroline St who was his uncle.[6] I told this boy that I intended making for Limerick Junction, which I understood to be the great rendez-vous for Munster, and that if I found nothing there I would try to go to America, and he was welcome to come with me, if so inclined. He agreed to join me.

We were not far from Mallow and about 7 o'clock – perhaps later, for it was dark – we entered a carman's stage near the railway viaduct, where we had the only substantial food since we left Cork. Owing to the seden- tary life I had led for the previous nine years I was not by any means robust, and if anyone had suggested to me that I should have to walk 35 miles without food or rest I should have thought it quite impossible that I could have endured it. My feet were well blistered – I had on my feet a new pair of strong boots which I had got made specially for the occasion and which I had not previously worn, which made walking more uncomfortable. However, I bathed my feet, rubbed them with lard, and had a sound sleep and was fit for the road again in the morning.

We passed Buttevant and Charleville. I made an attempt near Charleville to get a jaunting car with some samples of tea and sugar with which I might proceed on my journey as a Commercial Traveller.

We now held on our course towards Limerick Junction. We passed Kilmallock without interruption, but we were told that the roads around were patrolled by military and police who required all those they met to give an account of themselves.

About three miles from Kilmallock opposite the ruined castle of Fanstown, at a bend of the road, we came face to face with a troop of dragoons. Murphy and I darted into a large field on our left. The fence was broken down, the dragoons followed and of course easily came up with us. My person having been curiously examined by the quartermaster Sergeant Regan, my revolver was easily discovered and taken as prima facie evidence of disloyal intention; and Murphy acknowledging that he was in my company, we were conducted as prisoners to the Kilmallock police barrack.[7]

Thus did I, on the seventh March 1867, find myself in the grips of the law. There were six or eight police in the Barrack and perhaps eight or ten infantry soldiers. I was surrounded by the police and roughly hustled. One fellow struck me repeatedly with his kneed, holding me by my coat collar; others pulled at my arms, another catching hold my neckerchief nearly choked me by forcing his knuckles against my throat. Another caught me by the beard and pulled away from him a handful of it. Getting a hold of my voice for a moment I appealed to the soldiers who witnessed the brutal attack made upon me not to let me be murdered. No sign was made by the soldiers and my appeal served only to exasperate the police still more against me.

I do not remember what put an end of their attack upon me – possibly it was because I made no resistance – I saw how foolish it would be to give them any excuse for violence, and I suppose the presence of soldiers forbade the perpetration of any actual personal injury.

When the police had enjoyed the exercise of their ill feeling, they made an examination of my clothing and took from me everything they found upon me. They then shoved me into a small cell intended for a single prisoner: about 6 ft by 7ft having a plank-bed built in it, and a small form of stool. There I found some dozen persons – nearly as many as could get standing room in it.

An hour or so later I was taken out. In their first examination they had not found the belt which I wore under my clothes and in which I had my money. Now I was required to undress – evidently in their search for this belt which, of course, they soon found.

The police had doubtless been pumping the young chap Murphy. I had told him that I had the money in a belt. It was therefore clear to me that he had given that information to the police. He had however the grace not to disclose anything as to my personality. I gave the name of

James Walsh. The dozen or so of us passed that night in the small cell as well as we could and the next day we were sent on a long jaunting car to Limerick County prison.

There I made the acquaintance of Mr Eagar the Governor of that establishment. His ways were peculiar: he played the part of spy and detective as well as that of Governor. Every facility was given for the *manufacture* of witnesses. In my cell and when I was taking the hour's exercise in the yard many were afforded opportunities for observing me. I learned, after a while, to protect myself from such machination to some extent when in the cell; I could generally hear the footsteps approaching and I would turn my back to the door, in which there was a spy-hole; or I would bring my handkerchief before my face. But the exercise yard was commanded by windows at which I saw posted for observation of those in the yard several intended witnesses. Some would even be brought to see me in the cell.

One day Eagar came into my cell. He walked some steps beyond me and in scarcely audible tones uttered the name, 'O'Brien'. Up to that time I had not been identified. His intention evidently was to surprise me into an acknowledgement of my real name. In this however he did not succeed for I made no sign whatever.

This little piece of strategy was in my opinion discreditable to a man in the position of Governor of an important prison. I remember on 25th March climbing up to have a peep from the window of my cell – and the glimpse I caught of the distant hills, covered with snow, bathed in brilliant sunshine had an exhilarating effect upon me.

My identity having at length been established I was removed to County Cork jail in the early part of April. The change was an improvement. A Commissioner issued for the trial of all those taken prisoners for complicity in the rising was appointed to begin work on Cork on 2nd of May, and those in the County Jail were allowed to meet together in a large room, to consult with their solicitors and with each other for the purpose of preparing for their defence. And this opportunity for talking together was a delightful change from the previous solitary confinement.

It must have been before the trial that we were permitted to take exercise together. I never knew men in higher spirits under any circumstances. It must have been before the trial – for, after trial it is unlikely that we would have been left together. Those who had been sentenced to various terms of penal servitude were without delay passed on to Mountjoy Prison. They would certainly not have had the benefit of their little indulgences usually granted to those sentenced to death – such as improved diet, porter, tobacco, and less restraint during exercise – and being allowed to spend several hours together in the same room. This was the good fortune of the five who had been sentenced: to be hanged, drawn and quartered. I believe this is the only sentence for High Treason or levying war – with which we were charged.[8]

Two had already had this sentence passed upon them in Dublin: General Thomas F. Burke and Captain John McCafferty. Strange to say I am unable to recall the names of the four who stood in the dock with me – there was Captain John McClure; a young Irish Canadian (Kelly, I think), he was a Protestant; a man named Joyce from whom we would gladly have dissociated ourselves; the fourth I cannot recollect.[9] The five of us appeared together in the dock only once, as well as I remember. We were all charged with levying war; but four were taken in connection with Kilcloony Wood for Knockadoon, while I was connected with Ballynockin.[10] I suppose it was owing to this that I was tried separately and the other four together.

Chapter 8

Trial and Imprisonment, 1867–1869

Of my trial I have not much to say. There was no attempt made to connect me with the conspiracy. And, to business people in Cork – to whom I had become known during the previous four years, my presence in the dock was a surprise; for I had been a hard-working man and I had paid close attention to my business. The Ballynockin policemen swore manfully, for they had had plenty of opportunities for identifying me in the prisons.

The general tale was that they were attacked by 150 men – every man having a rifle and a knapsack. The sole foundations for the 150 knapsacks was a small hand bag to which I had got straps fixed and which was carried as a knapsack by a young man of the party. This gentleman was I believe a medical student. He has for many years been and still is a doctor in a town in Lancashire.

As I declared my inability to employ council Messieurs Caulfield Heron and Waters (now County Court Judge Waters) were assigned to my defence.[1] Mr Waters visited me in the County Prison to discuss the indictment. The most important point connected [with] the trial was the language of Judge Keogh in passing sentence – the complimentary terms in which he spoke of me. One phrase struck me as, under the circumstances, grotesque. He spoke of me as a man of *well-balanced mind*, I, having been a few minutes before found guilty of high treason and the circumstances showing conclusively that the attempted rising had not the least chance of success.

During the trial I was not quite at ease. I looked forward to the inevitable result with perfect equanimity. When asked whether I had anything to say why sentence should not be passed upon me, my remarks were few. I had prepared a speech dealing with the misgovernment of the country – and this as a matter of courtesy I gave to my solicitor, Michael Collins. When I wanted to get it back, he put me off from day to day saying it was in the hands of my Counsel and he would let me have it in good time. But he never returned it and when the time came I was quite unprepared to speak what I so much wished to say and felt considerably embarrassed in consequence. Sentence was passed in due form: that upon a certain day two or three weeks thence I was to be hanged, drawn and quartered. I believe this is the only sentence for high treason, and any other sentence would have been illegal. But the subsequent commutation of that sentence was not illegal.

Under sentence of death I was entitled to several indulgences and relaxation of discipline of which I availed very willingly. Among these relaxations were long visits from the chaplain to prepare me for death.

Alike had some days earlier been passed upon General Thomas F. Burke and Captain McCafferty in Dublin, and as far as I could gather no one expected that the sentence would be carried out. That was my impression in my own case also and the chaplain and I treated the sentence as a formality, as regarded the death penalty, so I enjoyed his visits and the visits of the few who ventured or cared to call on me – and they were few.

The other high treason trials were soon gone through and then the five of us were allowed to spend the day together at exercise in the open air or in a large room. We were all about 'as merry as cricket,' though upon what authority we accept the statement as to the merriment of cricket I do not in the least know. It reminds me of Rev. Dr Cahill, when in the fifties, was a remarkable man as a priest, a lecturer, a politician and a newspaper proprietor.[2] I remember attending lectures on electricity he delivered in aid of the new Presentation Convent in Dungarvan. He several times in the course of his lecture would say, 'If you ask me to give you a reason for this I can only tell you it is an ultimate fact.' In the same way – instead of raising questions as to whether crickets are merry or not I think we may accept it as an ultimate fact.

I am not able to say much about any of the Seven who were sentenced to death.[3] Burke I caught glimpses of a few times. The first time was in Mountjoy Prison. He was lame from wounds received in the great Civil War in the United States and apparently in a feeble condition of health. I think he was in the exercise ground at the time and I had only a glance of him through the open door. The next sight of him I had was on board the gun-boat which carried some thirty of us to Holyhead, chained in two gangs of fifteen each. Burke wore his beard full and long; he was about the middle height and I should say before he had been wounded he must have been active. I should say he was naturally of a very jolly and cheerful temperament, owing to the state of his health he was allowed or ventured to take more liberty of tongue than the rest for he spoke occasionally. I don't think the rest of us ventured to speak. We had spent the beginning of the Solitary Confinement period at Mountjoy – about six weeks or two months and the prison warders attended us, so that I think the prison discipline was maintained even on the gun-boat and the subsequent railway journey to Millbank Prison, London. After this I saw Burke a few times in Millbank, catching only a passing glimpse of him. I don't suppose he remained long at Millbank but was sent on to Dartmoor – where I think Kickham and other invalids were kept.

As well as I can recall I first saw Capt. McCafferty in Millbank. He also was lame from a wound received in the great American Civil War, but he was apparently in robust health. While Burke was on the side of the North, McCafferty was on the side of the South. I think he had served with Morgan's guerrillas.

McCafferty was I am confident a man of great courage and daring, and had the circumstances afforded him an opportunity he would have made his mark in a campaign for Ireland.

It lifts up my heart even now to think of the heroism – the splendid courage of our men! It was the most desperate of 'forlorn hopes,' but they went into it with light hearts and cool daring that could not be surpassed. And what is far more – they bore the penalty of long terms of penal servitude – the worst punishments in my opinion, that can be inflicted on men of active minds as we Irish are, with a quiet, uncomplaining endurance to the Will of God which was still more heroic.

Once McCafferty and I had a brief interview in Millbank Prison. Some sixty of more Fenian prisoners had been quartered at the prison, in Solitary Confinement, but some how the word passed around, in chapel I believe, that any of us who might prefer it would be sent to Western Australia where they would be employed making roads in the country, and be allowed considerable liberty. The contrast as compared with the solitary cell in Millbank was attractive, and I believe I was the only one who declined the offer. I declined because somehow I had convinced myself that my imprisonment would not be long and I thought that to be released in Western Australia, with empty pockets, while I had a mother and two children in Ireland would be worse than release in England.

McCafferty, whose American citizenship was recognised, I believe was not asked to go. The party of Fenian Prisoners was quartered together in adjoining corridors of the prison. And when they left the prison for Australia McCafferty and I were left in the exercise ground while cells in another part of the prison were being selected for us. McCafferty then proposed to me that we should refuse to submit to the prison discipline and take the consequences. But I pointed out to him that while I entirely approved of his suggestion, the fact that those who had been in prison since 1865 had submitted to the prison discipline made it impossible for us to take such a course. I entirely approved of O'Donovan Rossa's refusal to submit – but the others who were in the same prison with him by submitting condemned him.

We had but very few minutes together. And I don't think we had an opportunity for exchanging another word in Millbank. I did meet McCafferty once afterwards – but where I am unable to recall. I saw him about 1872 or 1873 in the city of Limerick at a distance. I and others were there about the business of the IRB. McCafferty was not I believe friendly to our views and came to Limerick to keep watch upon us – at least this was what was told to me. He thought himself incognito but I recognised him readily.

Captain McClure had also been in the Confederate Service. He was I should say about 25 years old in 1867 – hardly so old, for his beard and moustache were only in the incipient stage. In height he was rather less than more than 5ft 6in; round face, dark hair.[4] He was mild and unassuming. I don't remember to have seen him anywhere but in Co. Cork Prison. I heard little or nothing of him. He did not talk much. I think he and McCafferty and Burke were released in the beginning of 1869 and had to go to America at once. I understand he has since been successful as a bookseller and stationer in New York. I remember having exchanged letters with him many years ago (perhaps 20 years). I do not recollect the subject of correspondence.

Edward Kelly, as well as I remember, was with McClure at Kilcloony Wood – where Peter O'Neill Crawley was killed – whether they had anything to do with the attack on the Coastguard Station at Knockadown I do not recollect. Kelly I should say was 5ft 7 or 5 ft 8 in, pale, sallow, dark hair, face rather long, very little sign of beard. He was rather silent. I don't remember having seen him except in Co. Cork Prison and in the dock. My recollection is that he was released either before my release (4/03/1869) or about that time; and that he returned to North America, where he died some years ago.

The patriotism of the men I came in contact with in those years was of a very high standard. Without calculation or hesitation they gave themselves to the service of their country unreservedly. As in 1798 the material – the men – was of the very best and with anything like tolerable circumstances as to equipment and leaders they would have proved unconquerable.[5] I am inclined to think those who condemn the efforts of '98, '48 and '67 are not the kind of men who make great patriotic sacrifices, and their opinions on those events are deserving of no notice.

Was 1798 a failure? Would it have been better for Ireland that the Irishmen of that epoch had submitted unresistingly to the frightful atrocities practiced upon them and their families? The Insurrection, which was the object of Wolfe Tone, Lord Edward and the other leaders, was failed by the machinations of the English Government. Having with the assistance of Reynolds, Armstrong and other traitors and spies succeeding in arresting the leaders, the United men became a disorganised and almost helpless body – while the knowledge of their plans which the Government obtained through seizures of important papers as well as through the traitors and spies, forced the hand of the new leaders to premature action. From this point of view the Insurrection of Lord Edward Fitzgerald was a failure. But the Government had planned another insurrection – an insurrection of an unarmed peasantry driven to madness by tortures and outrages on family honor which no man can endure unresistingly and retain his manhood and self-respect. This insurrection was designed and manipulated by the Government with the intention that it would afford them an opportunity of so terrifying the people by massacres and devastating the country in all directions that no spirit would be left in Ireland to resist their scheme to the destruction of the Irish Parliament. The Government succeeded in their object, but had they realised the spirit their atrocities would arouse, in County Wexford for example, they would hardly have run the risk.

A competent general at the siege of New Ross would, under the providence of God, have entirely changed the fortunes of Ireland. For New Ross would have been quickly captured and 20,000 of the victorious Irish troops might easily have swept through Waterford, Kilkenny, Tipperary, Cork, Limerick etc., and the whole southern half of Ireland would have rallied to the fight.

Again – at Arklow – the battle was won and a competent general would have led his army at once to Dublin, inaugurating a provisional government who would call the whole country to arms. Or, had even a moderate body of French soldiers – with a good supply of arms and ammunition etc. been landed during the Wexford campaign there would have been a speedy end to English tyranny in Ireland.

But, even with all the accumulated horrors attending it, what Irishman to whom the honour of Ireland is dear, would venture to say – it would have better that there had been no insurrection in 1798 – and that it would have been better that our people had submitted unresistingly to the atrocities inflicted upon them? I cannot imagine such an Irishman! Had our people submitted unresistingly in 1798 the manhood of the country was lost – there would have been no Thomas Davis, no '48, no '67 and Ireland would be today the home of slaves and tyrants.

Ninety-eight, forty-eight and sixty-seven have given proof of the determination which I believe will *ever* be found in the hearts of the Irish people: that Ireland must be a self-governing country, and that the struggle for this sacred cause must be carried on by such means as may be available until success be attained.

The halcyon days – while we remained under sentence of death – quickly came to an end; and one morning I was notified that her majesty's clemency had been exercised in my case; that my sentence had been commuted to one of *Penal Servitude for life*. This at once impressed me with a sense of reality that the original sentence did not carry with it. And I felt that the only course for me was to submit without murmur or resigning to whatever was before me.

I think God for my sanguine temperament. In the worst state of things in which I may find myself I soon begin to see that things might have been worse – and to see reasons for bearing patiently – especially when the trouble follows from my own deliberate action. I was brought to a portion of the Prison I had not seen before – I had to resign my own clothes – to take a bath and to put on the prison dress of grey frieze. It looked to me as like the Irish workhouse dress, but it was highly respectable when compared with the English convict dress I later wore of coarse drab tweed – with its large black stripes and branded all over with the *broad arrow* in black, which makes one look like a tiger on two feet.

With the prison dress I was at once subjected to strict prison discipline. No more chumming now, no more friendly chats with my comrades. Indeed I think we were that very day removed to Mountjoy Prison, Dublin. Immediately after I had exchanged my own clothes for the prison dress my beard and hair were cut quite close, the first result of which was a severe cold and inflammation of the throat which made [deglutition?] and mastication impossible for about a week. The Mountjoy Prison Dr. (McConnell) told me if my beard and hair had not been cut off in Cork he would not allow it to be done in Mountjoy. He said he had not permitted General Burke's beard to be cut off.

I had nothing to complain of at Cork Prison or Mountjoy Prison. In each the diet was coarse but wholesome and quite sufficient in quantity for me – I am however a man of light weight – about 9½ stone – and a moderate eater; and a man of 12 or 14 stone would starve on the diet that would be abundant for me.[6] Of this I had man examples at Millbank and Portland Prisons.

I had nothing to complain of in the conduct of the Prison Officers at Cork or Mountjoy. In each Prison discipline was maintained without offensiveness. I spent two months or more in Mountjoy and probably about the end of August 1867 some thirty of us chained in two gangs of 15 in each were sent off to Holyhead in a gunboat.[7] Thence by train to London and that night we were introduced to Millbank. Another lot of 30 or more must have been drafter to Millbank about the same time. For I soon found that there were some seventy of us occupying two adjoining wards or corridors.

It was at Millbank we had our first experience of an English convict prison. Six or seven, or more, were brought into a corridor, we were ranged along by the wall at an interval or a few feet. We were ordered to strip naked, our clothes were removed (and carefully searched I have no doubt), each of us was then subjected to a very close and very disgusting examination of his whole person. I had to submit to a similar process four or five times at least during my time in Millbank and Portland. Of course it is utterly disgraceful that political prisoners should be so treated. The English People are aware of this and as the system could not be maintained without the approval of the Members of Parliament elected by them, they cannot repudiate responsibility for it. It has been carried on by Liberal and Radical Governments, as well as by Tory and Unionist Governments alike. It was no disgrace to us who had to submit to this treatment.

O'Donovan Rossa was right in refusing to submit to convict prison discipline in 1865, and if his comrades had taken the same course I think their resistance would have been successful. But as Rossa was alone in his resistance he was practically condemned by his comrades and he had no chance of success.

The impression made upon me by the officers at English Convict Prisons was that, with very few exceptions, they hated us. I believe the warders were specially selected as men who could be relied upon to treat us harshly. I am confident they were carrying out special instructions in our regard. I believe the desire of the Government was by their treatment of us to make such an example as would strike terror into the hearts of disaffected Irishmen. Such efforts failed in 1868 and in 1798.

My cell was about 9 feet long – from door to window – about 7 feet wide and 9 feet high. The floor was flagged, the bed was a sloped plank, at the foot about an inch from the floor – rising to about ten inches at the head – where there was in addition a box-like arrangement serving as pillow or bolster. I had a mattress to spread over the plank. It might have been better originally but when it came to me the material of coarse linen contained about as much chaff as I could hold in my two hands opened. The bed-clothes consisted of a sheet large enough to use under and over a blanket, and a rug. I found it much easier to endure the plank under my body than under my head. I managed tolerably however by putting my woollen cap under my head.

I found the cell very cold at night in winter. Indeed at times I was unable to sleep from cold, and I would get on my breaches and stocking and sit down with the bed-clothes huddled around me. If this had been discovered I have no doubt it would have been treated as a breach of prison rules and I would have been put on punishment diet. On such occasions how I long for the day light!

My sleeping place was unusually cold. I endeavoured to locate the position of my cell from the outside when taking exercise, and if I was right in my attempt, my cell was immediately over a large ventilator nearly as large as a window – this must have brought a constant flow of cold air under my bed. I made no complaint – I would not give them an excuse for saying something offensive – they were not going to select a specially warm cell for me.

The prison routine, as well as I can now recall it, was: turn out at 6 a.m., wash and remove slops, scrub stone floor of cell. Breakfast, 8 ounce badly baked bread and 3/4 pint cocoa. After breakfast to chapel for prayers, and after that to work in the cell. Warders go around – and, assisted by one of more convicts, give to each prisoner a quantity of old rope to be picked into [illegible]; or some old coir rope or matting to be teased or picked. For two reasons I always did my best at this work – work of almost any kind would at any time have been welcome to me as a relief from the pain of idleness, and now I had determined not to give my persecutors any excuse for trampling upon me or ill using me in any way. As far as rested with me there should be no excuse for subjecting me to any humiliating punishment; and what I could not avoid I had decided to submit to without complaint or murmur.

Of course prison officials are well aware that the capacity for doing such work as that given to me must be very different in the men they had to deal with – some being better adapted for it according to their previous occupations, while old prisoners who had acquired experience of all the prison ways had learned easy ways of doing this work. But they acted towards me as if they expected me to do as much as an old jail bird, and I was never able to satisfy them – or they took advantage of the opportunity thus afforded them, for every day I had to listen to complaints that I was not doing the proper amount of work, and that I should be reported. This barging and complaining went on every day.

While at work I sat on my bucket which was covered – I suffered considerably from pain in the back, and to get support for my back I moved the bucket near the wall. This soon caught the eye of one of the officials – and I was forbidden to put the bucket near the wall. The result of this was I contracted a disease of the spine which continued for many years.

About 1 o'clock we had dinner. It varied somewhat. Three days in the week we had 3 or 4 ounces of mutton (bone included) and one pound of potatoes and one day we had a kind of [illegible] consisting of all sorts of meat scraps made into a thick soup or stew. This was not unpalatable but it would have been much better relished but for the stories of what had been found in the mess.[8] On Friday we had duff, a sort of suet pudding – which I found difficult of digestion. Sunday dinner was ¼lb. Cheese and 12 ounces bread, and water.

On week days we had an hour for dinner – which left about half an hour for reading. Some tolerably good books were to be had – if you knew they were there and asked for them. One such book I got, having somehow heard of it, viz. Ranke's Lives of the Popes.[9] After dinner work was resumed. From 5 to 6 p.m. we had the hour exercise in the prison yard; and at 6pm supper of 6 ounces bread – badly baked – and a pint of gruel – supposed to be of oatmeal but I think it contained something else – for it appeared to be more like paste than oatmeal.

The exercise consisted of walking around the prison yard, in single file, at about 2 paces distance. Any attempt to communicated by word or sign was almost certain to be detected and was punished by bread and water diet and the dark cell. I once had 24 hours of this. It became known that a scrap of newspaper had been passed from hand to hand. Possibly we were all searched for it. I only know that I was searched and that it was found on me. I was taken to the dark cell. It was like an ordinary cell but that the window had been bricked up – as far as I was able to make out – the space that one brick would fill was left open to admit air. It did not admit light. My shoes, suspenders, pocket handkerchief and cap were taken from me. The bed was the usual plank bed. I don't think I had bed-clothes of any kind. I had bread and water diet for that day. I got through the 24 hours without caring much about it. I don't think anything they could have done to me would have disturbed me much, for I had always been willing to give my life for Ireland all I had gone through was less than that.

After supper there was nearly an hour for reading – then to bed – about 8.30. The prison exercise was occasionally varied, viz. by working at the Crank; but this was after our fellows had been shipped off to Western Australia – and as far as I knew only McCafferty and I remained at Millbank. How long after my interview with him (already described) he remained I had no means of knowing. The Crank was a pump for supplying water to the prison. Sixteen men worked together, eight at each side, so that the sixteen heads were close together. Such opportunity for conversation was availed of. The warders who stood 8 paces to the rear were supposed to prevent it but at such as distance they could hardly detect us and the noise of the machinery drowned or concealed the low-toned conversation.

I have mentioned my work of picking [illegible] and Coir. The sedentary position involved had become very irksome, and was having an injurious effect on my health in various ways, beyond the spine trouble. I was therefore glad to learn that I might get a change to occupation by asking to be put to mat-making. This was quite a relief, for the mat was made on a frame and I had constantly to change my position before the frame; stooping low and again standing up. At first it all was irksome, but I soon found it a change for the better, as I anticipated.

Millbank was an uneventful life. Solitary confinement is a severe strain on physical and mental health. Sometimes I felt alarmed at a sort of mental stagnation. The system is horrible and altogether abominable. Why it was ever adopted I am unable to understand. The natural outcome of it is to destroy men, mind and body – not a desirable consummation in my opinion. It would be more humane, less costly, and not more immoral to deprive convicts of their life in some summary way.

Having put in the full period of solitary confinement it was now time to send me off to the Public Works Prison. I believe the rule in England is eight months' solitary and, as well as I can run it out, I had been about 10 months at Millbank – while I had spent nearly two months at Mountjoy. Indeed except for ten or twelve days during my trial and my time after trial before Commutation of Sentence from hanging, drawing and quartering to penal servitude for life, my imprisonment from the first day at Limerick Jail had *all* been solitary confinement. So that, before I had been transferred to the Public Works Prison, I had really endured about fourteen months solitary.

I had some inkling of the coming change – how I cannot now remember. It might have been from the warder – or from the prisoner who assisted the warder in bring the coir for mat-making to my cell. I believe it would have been a matter of course for warder to talk of such a thing to the ordinary convict – but it was not so with me.

One morning I was ordered out of my cell and, having been led to a corridor, handcuffs were put upon my wrists, a chain running through a ring in the handcuffs united me to six others. We were then put into the Prison Van and driven to a Railway Station. We had to stand on the Platform for some ten minutes – all eyes fixed upon us. Of course we were in the regular prison dress: knee-breeches and jacket of coarse drab tweed having horizontal stripes of black an inch wide – and stamped all over with the broad arrow, the lower half of the leg encased in blue stockings having red stripes. And on the head a cap of same style of the stockings. I did not quite enjoy the wait at the Railway Station. I did not know where I was going; I only hoped it would be to Portland for I knew that Luby, O'Leary and other friends were there.

We were put into a third class carriage in charge of a number of warders. The journey was very long and wearing, and owing to the state of my health at the time I suffered much pain not being at liberty to leave the carriage for the ten hours or so. The chain and the handcuffs increased the discomforts. The end of the journey was Portland Prison – where I got a print of gruel and 8 ounces of bread before I could rest my weary back on my plank bed.

A curious place in which I saw Luby the second time in my life. The first time, I have already mentioned in due chronological order, was in 1849, on an Irish green hillside, at Carrickbeg, when we were both involved in Fintan Lalor's conspiracy. The second was in 1868 at the quarries of Portland Convict Prison.

In '49 I was in the full vigour of youth – ready to do and dare anything and everything for Ireland's sake and my hopes were unbounded. Strange to say the sight of O'Leary and Luby on my first introduction to Portland found me almost as light-hearted as I had ever been – though I had but just arrived having put in some ten months of solitary cells at Millbank on the journey to Portland had been one of a chained gang, all but myself ordinary convicts. The sight of those two was refreshing and comforting after ten months of the scowling faces of the brutal savages specially selected to degrade the Fenian prisoners at Millbank.

I forget how many of our men were then at Portland – nearly all were employed stone-dressing of a higher or lower class of work. Some were then preparing an altar and pulpit for the Catholic Chapel of some prison and among those on that job were Sergeant Charles McCarthy and Michael Regan. The work I was set to was preparing 'noblers': roughly squaring stones for a wall. This as well as a higher class of stone dressing was done upon a bank or stone bench, a large block of stone.

Our party worked in front of a shed in which we might take refuse when it rained. By some good fortune I was permitted to have my bank beside those of O'Leary and Luby. This was a great comfort to me – for conversation was almost unrestricted. Efforts were made to stop it whenever, as far as we could judge, political feeling was freshly exacerbated outside.

This arrangement afforded me an opportunity of learning something of the attitude of James Stephens towards his principal lieutenants.[10] I have endeavoured to give some idea of this elsewhere. According to Luby's statement Stephens had them in a condition little short of hypnotic subjection. He represented to them that he could surpass the greatest men of the past or the present taking the best work of each – whether painters, sculptors, architects, poets or other writers. And strange to say they accepted his estimate of himself. He had an idea of building a new city at Killarney, the architecture of which should harmonise with the surrounding scenery.

Such was Luby's statement in the presence of O'Leary – from which he did not dissent. It could not be expected that a man having such an opinion of himself should consult with men who took him at his own price.

Thomas Clarke Luby was at this time about forty years old, height about 5ft 4 in. Hair and beard were cropped close in prison – light sandy – rather fair. Small face, cheek bones a little prominent – chin somewhat pointed – nose rather large for the face and pointed. He had a comical habit of turning his head to one side when looking at you – that reminds me of a jackdaw. If at the same time there was on the [illegible] an amusing subject Luby's aspect was funny – for his eyes then had a comical twinkle.

I do not know what course he had read at Trinity. I think he was preparing for the bar. Not infrequently Luby and O'Leary would take up a religious topic – on which occasions Luby almost invariably took the Catholic side – O'Leary the anti-catholic side, but he did not adopt the views of any other religious denomination – to my mind his position was deplorable: he had lost the Catholic faith but had found nothing to replace it. He appeared to believe in God and Christ in a general way.[11]

As far as I can now recall Luby was born a Catholic – but when he was seven years old his father became a Protestant, and from that time he was sent to Protestant places of worship – in fact, became a Protestant with his father. His uncle was a Protestant and a Fellow of TCD and was I believe in good circumstances. I don't know whether the uncle had been born a Protestant or whether he had influenced the change in Luby's father.

It was at Portland Prison I learned from Luby the attitude of James Stephen towards himself, Leary and Kickham – which O'Leary at least tacitly acknowledged but which Kickham denied as far a he was himself concerned while he confirmed Luby's statement as far as Luby and O'Leary were concerned.

It was to the effect that Stephens posed as a genius of the highest order, combining in himself all the talents of practically all the greatest men who had gone before – I do not remember whether military genius was included in his great qualities but I presume it was, for it must have been on this ground that no one presumed to question his decisions regarding the affairs of the IRB.

It would appear that Stephens had acquired a complete ascendancy over the minds of Luby and O'Leary – and also I have no doubt over the other men who came into close touch with him since, to my mind, Luby and O'Leary were men of higher intelligence than the others – Kickham excepted.

During those conversations at Portland they very strongly censured Stephens's management – but Luby remarked that: if they were released tomorrow and came within reach of Stephens's influence it was very likely that he would regain his power over them!

Luby once told a curious story about himself – before his marriage. He was one day walking with a friend when he saw before them the future Mrs L. The two gentlemen followed her for some distance until she disappeared into her own house. They ascended the steps of the house about half a minute later. They found the young lady already divested of her walking apparel. Luby remarked on the rapidity of the change and asked her where she had been. But she assured them that she had not been out of the house recently.

I found Luby a most agreeable conversationalist and a very likeable man. In 1870 after my second marriage I lived in Dublin for some time and then I became acquainted with Mrs Luby and her children: two boys and a girl. Mrs Luby was under the middle height – about 5 feet – face round, hair very fair, agreeable expression, manner very quiet and sedate in fact, just the wife Luby needed to steady him is what I thought.

They lived in a small house at Dolphinsbarn. Luby's mother – to whom he was much attached – was one of the family. The two boys as well as I remember were darker than the mother – but quiet-mannered like her – while the daughter was nearly as fair as the mother while she was more like her father in manner: light-hearted and jolly. She was then only about ten years of age.[12]

Of the men (Fenians or IRB) whom I met at Portland Prison one was distinctly insane, while a second was apparently on the border line. The name of the first I do not remember nor do I recollect whether I subsequently heard what had become of him. I was told that he had been a corn porter in Dublin. He was a fine, tall, well-built man, about 6 ft. high.

It is quite possible that his mental disease was due to semi-starvation – and ill-nourished body resulting in a starved and diseased mind. The poor fellow was under the delusion that his fellow prisoners had entered into a conspiracy to murder him. It was pitiable to observe his attitude towards the rest of the little party. He was watchful and ever on his guard lest he should be taken by surprise. He spoke very seldom, and very little.

The name of the second man I remember quite well – but as I trust that he regained his mental equilibrium after his release from prison I think it would be injudicious to name him. He was an excellent man and was perhaps the best hand – among the party – in the stone work for altars and pulpits. He was a very devout Catholic, and he appeared to take a decided pleasure in the work that was intended to be used for Catholic worship.

The conduct of the prison officials during my time in Portland was unintelligible. Generally we were allowed to converse with restraint, but occasionally the warders became quite tyrannical – we were forbidden to talk – and necessary communication connected with the work had to be made through warders. We were usually allowed to assist each other in moving large stones to or from our banks; but on one occasion this was prohibited, and while moving a stone to my bank it fell upon another, caught one of my fingers and took the top of it off. The finder took about a fortnight to heal and before it had quite healed the Governor of the prison insisted that I should resume the scrubbing of my cell –

which I had been discontinued when my finger got hurt. I however refused to comply – and learning that the Prison Inspector – Captain Fagan – was expected soon I gave notice to the Governor that I would bring the matter before the Inspector. This I did – and to my surprise and gratification Captain Fagan turned to the Governor who sat beside him, and said, 'The Governor will see that this does not happen again.' I was not again asked to scrub my cell.

It was not long after this, perhaps a month or more, that I was amnestied. It was the 4th of March 1869. A warder came one day to the quarries where we worked. The day had been wet. We were at the time were working in the shed. The warder called out from a paper in his hand the names of five prisoners. The first name was James Walsh, but no one answered to that name. I guessed it meant myself – for that was the name I gave when I was arrested. I did not however venture to make any observation lest I should be mistaken and though I had nothing upon which to based my supposition – beyond the fact that, for some short time previously we had been harshly treated, yet the idea came to me that those who were called were about to be released.

Having called the five names and four having replied the warder again called, 'James Walsh *alias* O'Brien' and then I answered: here. We were then desired to leave our work, and having advanced to where the warder stood – he told us we were wanted at the Governor's Office: and, telling us to follow him, he set off.

As far as I could see none of the other four men had any suspicion as to the reason of our being sent for; but the idea was so strong in my mind that even at the risk of being mistaken I ventured to convey my suspicion to them, for the purpose of warning them in case my expectations were realised – to control features and tongues and not to indulge in any signs of rejoicing – and, above all, to offer no thanks to the Governor.

It proved that I was right. We were all five led into the Governor's Office, he sitting at a high desk and we standing immediately before the desk; the Governor read out from a paper the instructions he had received from the Home Office to the effect that a free pardon had been extended to each of us and we were to be released at once.

Having read this the Governor raised his head and looked at us – evidently expecting to see us beside ourselves with joy, and he no doubt ready to receive our thanks. He was certainly astounded! This was clearly visible in his face – when he saw us standing before him without a word, a sign or emotion of any kind.

Seven, I think, were released that day: five from Portland, and two from Dartmoor, Kickham and another whose name I do not remember. I cannot at present call to mind the names of the four who left Portland Prison with me.

At times I recall the past distinctly but my recollection is not always equally clear. As well as I remember two took train for London and two others with me set out for the south of Ireland via Bristol. A suit of clothes and about three pounds were given to each of us. I remember I gave an equal sum of money for the poor through the Sisters of Charity on my arrival in Cork.

The clothes given us were I believe the same as were supplied to released convicts and taken in conjunction with our closely cropped heads, and faces – the beard was cut closely with scissors – and our generally unkempt condition I have no doubt we were easily recognised as released jail birds. It certainly appeared to us that we were looked upon with suspicion at the Hotel in Bristol at which we put up. And this was but natural under the circumstances.

As to how we felt on getting outside the prison – my recollection is that my companions behaved like boys who had unexpectedly been let out for a holiday with a little money in their pockets. I don't remember that at any time in my boyhoods' days I ever frolicked like others; and I certainly did not on this occasion. Somehow life has always felt serious to me and while I felt happy it was in a quiet, serious way.

Chapter 9

1869–1874

_____

From Bristol two I think went by steamer to Cork, but I went to Waterford. My cousin Rev. Dr Cleary (now Archbishop of Kingston, Canada) was then the President or vice-president of St John's College, Waterford. He met me at the steamboat landing and brought me at once to the Presentation Convent (one of my sisters was a member of that order – in another town). And there I found the suit of my clothes which I wore during my trial and up to the day when after conviction and sentence I was deprived of my clothes and my hair and beard removed closely. In the Convent I was afforded an opportunity for donning my own clothes and making a hasty toilet.

I was next made partake of the hospitality of the Convent, after which I was introduced to every member of the Community. If I had been the favourite brother of each of the nuns my welcome could not have been warmer or more kindly.

Circumstances led me to visit many Convents in various parts of Ireland, in that and subsequent years, and everywhere the Fenian who had given proof of his desire to serve Ireland met the same warm-hearted reception. God bless our Irish Nuns! Meet them at home or abroad – in Foreign Convents – their hearts always beat warmly for Ireland and for those who love Ireland.

After I had been well refreshed Dr Cleary drove me about Waterford in his own trap and introduced me to some of his friends. During these troublous times a Committee existed which collected money to make provisions for Political Prisoners on their release. My feeling on this subject was that there were many of the prisoners whose need of such assistance was greater than mine, for while I had not a penny I could call my own, I could at once to go work and provide for my wants. Many others would not be in so favourable a position. I therefore declined to accept anything from this Committee and I borrowed £10 from Dr Cleary to provide for immediate necessities.

I now went to Cork where I was received with a triumphal procession, band or bands, etc. It was just two years after my arrest in '67. I immediately engaged to go to work for the firm of Messieurs James Clery and Co, for whom I had been doing business up to the night of the 'rising'. While I was previously Manager my occupation was necessarily sedentary and within doors; in order to recruit my health, which of course had suffered from the harsh imprisonment – as well as for another reason which influenced me much more and which will soon be apparent – I now decided to take up the work of Commercial Traveller for the firm for a time.

The week that intervened was by no means an idle week for me for almost immediately after my return to Cork I had interviews with representative men connected with the IRB organisation in Munster, and very soon with men outside Munster. From these I was delighted to learn that the collapse of '67 had not at all disheartened the men of the Organisation, and that it still maintained its ranks unbroken. The work of the IRB was now carried on by a Supreme Council. Without hesitation I at once threw in my lot with the Organisation as I found it; and I decided to take every advantage of the facilities my position as Commercial Traveller afforded me for advancing the interests of the IRB

The ground I travelled over included the whole of Munster, the greater of Connaught, portions of Meath, Kings and Queens Counties, Carlow, Kilkenny, Kildare, Wicklow and Wexford – I may say all Ireland except Ulster.

I found the IRB Organisation vigorous and healthy almost everywhere. If a plebiscite could have been taken then or within the following few yeas, it would have been found that the vast mass of the men – aye and of the women of Ireland – were heart and soul strongly in sympathy with the IRB – that is: in favour of an Irish Republic.

I think I never met anyone so unfit for the duties of a Commercial Traveller as myself; and if my success or failure had depended on my natural fitness for the position I should quickly have proved a complete failure. I felt my unfitness painfully – but a fair amount of business was obtained for me through the good offices of the men of the IRB, some of whom were in business in almost every town while others had influence with the people in business. And the people who gave me orders for goods gave them either as IRB men or as sympathisers or at least in recognition of the power and strength of the Organisation. In this way I extended the operations of the Cork firm far beyond the limits to which they had previously been confined.

Some two months after I began work as Commercial Traveller I visited Mullinahone where resided C. J. Kickham. Kickham had been released from Dartmoor Prison the same day I was released from Portland but we had never met before my visit to Mullinahone.

As far as I understand Dartmoor was the prison for invalids. As for poor Kickham's health, not only was his digestion much impaired, but his sight was very defective and he could scarcely hear a cannon shot. Conversation with had therefore to be carried on upon the fingers as with the death and dumb. He also had, immediately after his release from prison, re-joined the IRB. I admired and liked him very much and I enjoyed his conversation greatly.

After my first visit to Mullinahone and my exchange of views with Kickham, I travelled through the greater part of the County of Tipperary, and probably about July or August (I remember distinctly it was summer), I arrived at Roscrea Railway Station before noon. I there met Mr Denis Caulfield Heron – who had been my leading counsel on my trial.

I learned from Mr Heron that there was then a vacancy for the Parliamentary representation of Tipperary and that he was there about to begin a canvas for the County. He asked me to 'put in a good word for him,' to which I made no reply. We occupied the same car from Roscrea Station to Brown's Hotel in that town. I made no delay at Roscrea, but went on to Nenagh, putting up at Syman's Hotel.

I had not been long here when a number of the young men of the town and the country around called to see me – it happened to be a market day. About twenty were present. One of the party, but no longer a young man, was Peter Gill, a very remarkable man he was – but my knowledge and experience of him are quite inadequate to attempt a description of him. He was then proprietor and conductor of a newspaper published at Nenagh. I am not quite sure of the name of the paper but I think it was 'The Nenagh Guardian.'[1]

In political matters Peter Gill was for years quite a power in Tipperary – in the northern half especially. How many Parliamentary elections he contested I cannot say – but I think he did contest several and I think he was always in the National Camp – in the sense that he was always, at least, a sympathiser, if not an active supporter of the National programme that happened to be prominent at each epoch from 1840 – or earlier – to the day of his death.[2]

My visitors – to whom it is time for me to return – remained about an hour, talking of the general politics of the day –especially that phase of politics with which I was known to be connected – and because of which, and to show their sympathy with which, they had called on me. Among other matters the vacancy for the Parliamentary representation was touched upon. Peter Gill suggested that O'Donovan Rossa ought to be put forward. No one, however, appeared to take an notice of this suggestion, but it struck me at once as a very good idea. And the young men having gone away – I turned to Peter Gill, who remained, saying: 'I have been thinking of your suggestion of starting Rossa for Tipperary; I think it is an excellent idea. From what I have seen – having just travelled through a large portion of the country – I believe it can be made a success.'

Peter was quite pleased that I had taken up his suggestion, to which I believe he had not given a moment's thought. 'Sit down,' I said, 'and draft something that will serve as Rossa's address to the electors.' Peter excused himself for this saying he could make a speech as long as desired but did not feel equal to the writing. Thereupon – having got pens, ink and paper – I wrote it myself. This production was denounced in the *Times* a little later as a rhapsody.

I must give here some explanation for having put forward O'Donovan Rossa's name on this occasion. He was at that time in an English convict prison – and most brutally treated. By some means he was able to send out from the prison a letter or scraps of paper containing an account of his treatment: for 17 nights and days I think his hands had been secured behind his back. The manacles were not loosed even to allow him to partake of the food put before him; he had therefore to take his food by lapping it like a dog.

The matter was brought before Parliament and of course the story was denied – scouted in the most indignantly virtuous manner by the Government officers of the day – I suppose the Home Secretary first – possibly supported by the Attorney General etc as is still the custom. An inquiry however was promised – upon which were to be employed – as well as I remember – one or more independent medical men.

I think the result of this inquiry had been made public a little before the time I am dealing with – and it practically confirmed Rossa's account of his most infamous treatment.

Needless to say all Ireland was filled with indignation in consequence of this brutal savagery on the part of the English Government. And I felt convinced that Rossa's election for Tipperary would be carried upon a wave of enthusiasm that would sweep the county from north to south.

I sent copies of 'Rossa's Address' to Cork and Dublin to be printed: I wished to make sure that if a hitch occurred in one place the work would be done in the other place. The next step was how to distribute the address all over the country and start the right men at the work of canvassing, etc. Upon this Peter told me the right man to get hold of was Daniel O'Connell, a young farmer from near Toomavara a few miles from Nenagh. Dan had not long been released from prison, I think he had been more than a year confined as a suspect.

Peter said Dan was certain to be in town at the market – and he sent someone, or possibly several persons, to look for him. He turned up very soon, and he entered most heartily into the idea of starting Rossa for the county, and to set the work going he undertook to go through the county and pass the word around.

We next made a list of those to whom [illegible] of the Address should be sent from Cork and Dublin. And to complete the first Act in the performance, we inaugurated a collection for defraying the expenses of the election by sending £6 to the Dublin newspaper The Irishman, being £1 from Dan O'Connell and £5 from myself.

The result of the election entirely realised my expectations.

Perhaps I ought to say here, that, in starting this election I went beyond the duties of the position I had lately taken up in the IRB Organisation, and I ought to have consulted my colleagues before taking such a step. There was, however, no time for consultation; not a day to be lost, the decision was to be taken that evening at Nenagh or not at all. Had there been time for consultation it was quite possible Rossa would not have been started, for having promptly informed Kickham of what I had done he did not approve of it – considering that it could not be made a success. I however having recently travelled through the country was better able to gauge the state of feeling.

Imagine what must have been the chagrin of poor Mr Heron, when he learned what I had done on the evening of that day, on the morning of which he asked me to 'put in a good word for him.'

A few days after this I received a letter from a man who at that time was a very prominent figure in Irish political life – I mean Rev. Patrick Lavelle – the PP of Partry in the Co. Mayo.[3] Father Lavelle was a much more remarkable and important man than Peter Gill. Peter was to some extent a power in the northern part of Tipperary, but Father Lavelle's power and influence, which were almost paramount in Mayo and largely in Galway, were recognised to a considerable extent over a great part of Ireland. He had also much influence among the Irish in America.

At this time I think Father Lavelle almost looked upon himself as the ruling power in National affairs. At all events, his letter referring to Rossa's candidature stated that: he had settled the matter; that Mr Heron had agreed to give £500 to the Ladies Committee and that Rossa was to be withdrawn. The Ladies Committee had been organised for the purpose of collecting funds for the support of the families of the Political Prisoners.

To Father Lavelle's letter I replied, that: 'Rossa cannot be withdrawn – not for a million!'

Of course Rossa's election was set aside, the Government Officers declaring him ineligible. And a new election was ordered.[4]

The Supreme Council of the IRB having foreseen this, considered what was advisable to be done in the approaching election, and came to the conclusion that a repetition of the tactics practiced in putting forward O'Donovan Rossa would be unmeaning and consequently they would not interfere in the coming election. I was authorised to make this known where necessary.

One result of the Rossa Election was to make evident how readily the funds necessary were subscribed by our friends. And this I think induced a number of young men in some of the town in Tipperary to take it upon themselves to start Kickham as a candidate in the new Election. I suppose they did not know that Kickham was himself a party to the understanding agreed upon by the Supreme Council. Such was the case however.

Of course under the circumstances the action of the young men was not supported by the recognised representatives of the IRB and notwithstanding the very great popularity of the name of Kickham, the desire to compliment him was not sufficient to make up for the diminished support in consequence of abstentions due to the spirit of discipline in those places in which I thought it safe to make known the views of the Supreme Council. It was much to be regretted that Kickham's name should have been used under such circumstances. A majority of votes was not cast for Kickham. I forget who was the other candidate, and I think the money contributed was not sufficient to defray the expenses – but of this I am not quite clear now.

I think it was in the early autumn of 1869 that my business brought me to Tuam. And finding that I was not far from Partry, Father Lavelle's parish, I made up my mind to visit him. When I had travelled about half the distance I learned that Fr Lavelle was then on the way to Cong to attend the Month's Mind of the late PP of Cong and the Neale: Very Rev. Dean Waldron. So, for Cong I altered my course. I soon was introduced to Fr Lavelle and by him I was invited to the dinner which was being prepared at the Hotel for the priests of the Deanery who attended the Month's Mind. I was then introduced to all the priests who were present – about twenty or more.

Father Lavelle was I should say not more than 5 feet high – round full face, eyes large, black, prominent, bold; hair black, curly, abundant.

A masterful little man, and combative, as was well known to every one who took an interest in Irish affairs of the period.

I believe on that day Fr Lavelle had ceased to be PP of Partry, having been appointed to succeed the late Dean Waldron as PP of Cong and The Neale. Of all the priests whom I met that day there was one with whom I at once became very friendly, Fr John O'Malley then CC of The Neale; later PP of The Neale when the two parishes were again separated. I visited Fr John after this whenever my business brought me anywhere near him. He always had a bed and a welcome for me.

I remember one winter night about 10 o'clock, very hungry after a long drive, Fr John had nothing to put before me to eat but some spare, *very* spare ribs of mutton that remained from the day's dinner. My performance upon those ribs made a lively impression upon Fr John – as for nearly twenty-two years (he died, God rest his soul, 30 May 1892) he was ever ready to joke me on that subject.

What a contrast he was to the new PP! Fr Lavelle was small and very dark – Fr John about 6 ft. 2 in., squarely built, very fair. They were both ardent Nationalists – warm sympathisers with the IRB movement. Indeed Fr John was a good deal more than a sympathiser – for he was a very active supporter. For years before this and for years after they were close friends. In the diocese they were among the priests called Ajax and Agamemnon.

Fr Lavelle's fame and influence were at this time widespread. In his own narrower sphere Fr John's influence was much greater. His relations with the people of Cong and The Neale were much more intimate than were Fr Lavelle's. In politics the people of the parish – and of some surrounding parishes also, I venture to say, accepted him as their leader. His rule was almost military. What a soldier he would have made!

Fr Lavelle's fame was of course well know to the more educated people of the district but it had not penetrated to the lower station. And I think he was looked upon by the uneducated as Fr John's subordinate.

I had not made many visits to The Neale before I met Fr John's sister – Maria O'Malley. We met afterwards at The Neale and at her home in Castlebar, as often as my avocations afforded me the opportunity – until one day: December 20 1870 – we met again, no more to part. For on that day we were married by Fr Lavelle in the chapel of The Neale – a wretched, thatched cabin not fit for a decent horse – much less for a place of worship. It was a survival of the bad old days of persecution and humiliation so long endured in suffering and sorrow by Catholics in Ireland.

When Father John was appointed PP of The Neale he, in the course of a few years, built a decent church in the most conspicuous part of the parish – the old thatched building was hidden away in a hollow. He also built three large commodious schools. He was a man of energy and action.

Of my marriage with Maria O'Malley I will only say – few men have been blest with a better wife; and perhaps fewer still have enjoyed a happier married life.

Upon the occasion of my marriage, Kickham gave proof of his friendship. Notwithstanding his disabilities (which indeed he did not appear to regard much) he consented to assist as my 'best man' at my marriage. He joined me at Thurles. A portion of our journey was by a small covered car for about three hours – and in the dark. Here was a prospect of total suspension of conversation for those three hours which we both disliked exceedingly – But I thought I would make an experiment and so taking Kickham's hand in mine I tried to practice the dumb alphabet, whereupon he burst out in ecstasy, 'No one ever thought of this before!' And we got through our journey very much more to our satisfaction than we anticipated.

There is little eventful to record in my life for some years. I continued my occupations as Commercial Traveller – though I utterly detested it – that I was not entirely unsuccessful was due to the friends who canvassed for orders for me.

My position was of course one of danger, for while I carried on the Organisation of the IRB I had also to keep up correspondence with the Secretary in Dublin, and with various persons in various places – my address of course changing every day. In guarding against danger from this source I had to be very watchful: calling at every address I had given and leaving instructions where to forward letters – and these came not only to my own name – but, the most important of them to other names (fictitious); and I think I was in the entirety successful.

Perhaps I might mention here a curious instance of correspondence getting astray or mixed up. Having returned to Dublin from the country at the end of a business round, I had a visit from the Secretary of the Supreme Council. I can see no reason why I may not mention his name as he died years ago – John Nolan (well known far and wide at the time as *Amnesty Nolan* for his untiring effort in that good cause).[5] Nolan had received a few days before a letter that puzzled him very much. I am inclined to think he must have known who was the writer, and for whom the letter was intended, but as the document which was written by one member of the Council and addressed to another, contained an incitement to cast out of the Council myself and other colleagues, John Nolan appeared to feel relieved when he had place the document in my hands. I had met the writer of the letter in the country a few days before, and among other subjects we discussed was the Protestant Home Rule Association, to which I found this gentleman strongly opposed.[6] I had expressed my views to the effect that I was well pleased to see it started, and would be glad to see it take hold in the country – that I felt convinced that those who might join that association would inevitably be carried farther when they would come to understand the shocking misgovernment of our country.

During our interview Mr —— did not dissent from anything I said, but rather left me under the impression that he agreed with me; but in the *mixed up* letter (it seems that Mr —— was writing to John Nolan and the other gentleman at the same time and placed the letters in the wrong envelopes) he ridiculed what I said on the subject as 'tawdry nonsense.' His opposition to the Protestant Home Rule Association was so strong that he wished that they should not be allowed to hold meetings and that organised efforts should be made to break up their meetings in case they attempted to hold any.

Singular to say, this gentleman – not many months later – became a shining light in the Protestant Home Rule Association. The gentleman in question is a man of great ability – self-educated almost. At the age of perhaps 28yrs recognising certain deficiencies he entered college to improve himself and he managed to pay his way by lecturing – a brave and manly thing to do. He has since made his mark to a certain extent, but with his capacity and abilities he might easily do much more.

His one weakness – obvious to me, he may have others also – is that he has made himself distrusted by those with whom he has worked. Of course he knows his own value – perhaps too well – and apparently he thinks himself better suited to leading positions than those who hold them. If he had been *straight* and bided his time he would I believe ere this have been a leading Irish Nationalist – if not *the* leading one.

During the four years or so that I spent going through the country as a Commercial Traveller – 1869 to 1873 – my comings and goings were carefully noted by the police. Some times I would make one town my headquarters for a week visiting neighbouring towns by car. On such occasions the police would try to learn from my driver what way I intended to go that day. I was frequently followed by policemen on another car. When I had gone into a shop on business, soon a policeman would come in to ask some trivial question or ask for change for a piece of silver or gold. But I took no notice of these tactics.

During those years I was a kind of public character and many persons desired to meet me in addition to those whom I met on the business of the IRB. And I had no difficulty in meeting the latter – at my hotel, if necessary in my bedroom, or at the private residence of friends of the cause.

Of course during those years I had very little home life, for which I always had a longing. Whenever possible I returned home at the end of the week but I was generally two and sometimes three weeks from home.

One Saturday I made a rush for the latest train for Dublin. I was then at Ennis. When I arrived at the station the train was in motion – but desiring the porter to shove in my luggage I jumped on the footboard on which I had to rest to recover breath – and with no little difficulty I cambered into the carriage, the speed of the train having gradually increased. There was no one in the compartment to help me – so that I was in no little danger when the train passed under a bridge before I had got in.[7]

A secret organisation that must be kept up for a number of years has in itself sources of weakness tending to disintegration. I should say the IRB was at its full strength, vigour and activity up to 1871. It was unavoidable but still regrettable that public houses were almost the only places in which the men could without suspicion meet each other.

I have observed various instances of men truly patriotic who would be delighted and proud to lay down their lives for the cause – yet it was strange to me at all events, to see how close-fisted those men could be when it became a question of parting with a little money – even when they were able to spare it. So that many placed a higher value on their money than on their lives. But what was much worse, in my rounds I learned of many instances of men who had given indisputable proofs of their devotion to the cause – making away with sums of money belonging to the Organisation which had been entrusted to them for safe keeping.[8]

The work of the IRB during those years was chiefly importing rifles and revolvers with the necessary ammunition – by every kind of secret means that could be devised. This of course was attended with no little risk. It was for his share in this work that Michael Davitt suffered some nine year or more of penal servitude.

Of course one cannot repress his indignation at the thought of the savageries to which Mr Davitt was subjected, but if it was necessary for his development into the important factor in Irish political life he has since become, I do not think the price was too high, even from the personal point of view.[9]

It was in 1870, as well as I remember, that I first met Mr Davitt, in connection with the purchase of arms in England and sending them to Ireland. I have no intention of venturing on a sketch of Mr Davitt. There are several who are much better acquainted with his life and services to Ireland than I – and who moreover are far more competent to deal with so important a subject.

My position in connection with the IRB during those years was one of considerable responsibility and needless to say full of anxieties. I felt that I was every day living over a mine that at any moment might explode under me. Even the miscarriage of a single letter might lead to my prompt arrest; and in the effort to avoid such dangers my mind was ever on the stretch ever on the alert. I might almost say that during those years I slept with one eye open.

About 1873 the signs of disorganisation and disintegration became more evident. I had to visit Cork in consequence of a sort of cave formed by some of the best men there. Having learned who was the proper person to summon a meeting of the leading men, I sought him myself – and after some difficulty I found him in a small public house. He professed himself afraid of a certain party who belonged to the cave. I however prevailed on him. And the meeting came off, and the ranks of the organisation were again reformed, a few of those who were tired of the business dropping out.

I remember how at this meeting a certain man – a plasterer by trade – one of those who wished to break up the organisation then – remonstrated with me stating that I would go on if I had but one man with me. Indeed at this time I was considering the desirability of restricting the organisation to a skeleton composed of the best of the officers – for I felt confident that whenever circumstances made it possible for us to take action the men of the rank and file, indeed the men of all Ireland, could very quickly be rallied.

I am of the same opinion still. This is one of the gross illusions of our task masters: that as Ireland is quiescent the people have given up their hostility to the enemies of their country. Nothing less than giving the Irish people the management of their own affairs will in the least degree appease their longing for recognition *as a Nation*. Nothing less can the slightest change of disarming the hostility of England. While their longing remains unsatisfied Ireland will welcome everything that threatens danger to England.

And further – the longer Ireland is quiescent the more easily will she be roused to physical force action. It required a great effort to induce them to give heed to Parnell's moral force tactics. Indeed while giving him a trial, they in a manner kept a hand on the sword all the time. They said to themselves, we can always fall back on the other.

The weariness of the long period of unrest in the ranks of the Organisation to which I have adverted – helped to secure a hearing for Parnell. The time was favourable for him, as had been for James Stephens the long period of rest from agitation from 1849 to 1859.

In the autumn of 1873 I think it was that I went to live at Cork. I was glad to give up the Commercial Traveller's life. I became accountant to the Cork Gas Company which brought me into close touch with a man whom I had long admired: Mr Denny Lane, the Secretary of the Company. He was one of that brilliant band of young men who rallied to O'Connell's side in the 'Forties'; and later felt compelled to object to the manner in which affairs were carried on at Conciliation Hall by the great man's entourage, and for which his son John O'Connell was chiefly blamed.

Indeed it is most likely that O'Connell's mind had already begun to suffer from the disease that after his death it was found had attacked the brain, and he was not accountable for what had been done in his name. The revolt of the young men against the action of John O'Connell gave rise to the 'Young Irelanders,' and 'Fortyeight Men' by both of which they are still known.

Some ten years earlier I made an occasion for calling at the Gas Office for the purpose of having a good look at Mr Lane. He was then in the prime of life possibly 45 years old. His head was covered with an abundance of black hair, which he wore rather long; beard and moustache also black. He was a fine-looking man, his height I should say was over 6 ft. He was well educated his mind was well stored from extensive reading.

He did not take a very active part in political affairs even in 1848. After that he had but little to do with politics. Like most of the 'Fortyeight Men' he thought it presumptuous on the part of those who entered the field of politics in the Fenian era. It is curious to observe how this game is played generation after generation: the veterans of the earlier day looking down with disapproval and an air of superior wisdom over those who have learned from them, and who in their youthful self-confidence think they can better their teachers. I suppose this is human nature, for it has been always observed in old and young soldiers and sailors also.

Denny Lane had a very active mind: always occupied with inventions and theories. He was an able Gas Engineer and was I believe equally skilled in Electricity. He started a brewery and a starch factory, both of which were I believe successful; but I rather think he was much more of a theoretical than a practical man.

I think it was in 1874 he was prevailed upon to become a candidate for the Parliamentary representation of the city of Cork. He was a fine speaker and he would have been a credit to Ireland as well as to Cork. There certainly was a striking contrast between his speeches on that occasion and those of his opponent Mr John Daly the draper.

I think it was about two years ago that I last met Mr Lane – I was walking towards the House of Commons from Trafalgar Square when we met. I think he was then on his way home to Cork – having attended a conference in France of the Gas Engineers of various countries. But he was delighted with the conference, where it appears, he was made much of. He had been called on to respond to 'a toast' on behalf of the Gas Engineers of Ireland; and as we walked along Charing Cross, Whitehall and Parliament Street he recited for me, in French, the speech he delivered on that occasion. In it he reminded the Frenchmen of the old friendship that existed between Ireland and France; many hard fought fields on which the men of the Irish Brigades were brothers in arms of the French soldiers of those great days. He told me of the enthusiasm his speech kindled among the Frenchmen and their amazement and the [flaming?] of his harangue.

Lane made a fine picture on that occasion – I don't think I ever before noticed his hair so long – it almost floated on his shoulders as he strode along. It was no longer quite black, for it was much sprinkled with grey hairs – as was his beard. Then the way he flung his arms about and gesticulated was splendid. If this scene had taken place in a smaller city, Dublin or Cork for instance, I am sure we should have had an admiring crowd about us; but in London one might do almost anything unless it were a breach of the law without attracting the notice of passers-by. Though at the same time I have frequently noticed how easy it is to attract notice and gather a crowd in London streets.

I think Mr Lane felt quite as much pleasure in telling me of the remark of one of his daughters, made when he had described them the scene he rehearsed for me. 'Oh papa I know what the Frenchmen were so amazed at – it was your bad French.' And he laughed heartily when he repeated to me this joke – that it looked as if the whole story were told for the purpose of quoting this joke. He was very fond of his children.

I think it was in the month of December 1874 that I decided to retire from the IRB. I have already said that the principal work we had been doing – at very great risk to the men engaged in that work – was importing rifles and revolvers. In my journeying through the country I found that practically useless; there was great difficulty in keeping them, and they were generally hidden away in places were they rapidly decayed, and became worthless. They could not be occasionally examined and cleaned without serious danger. I came to the conclusion that we were paying too high a price for such worthless work. We were taking money from our men to pay for these useless arms.

It was therefore gradually borne in upon me that the IRB had ceased to be a useful organisation. Confidence in it had almost ceased. Of course this did not come upon me all of a sudden – it forced itself upon my gradually; but at length I concluded that it would be wrong for me to continue in the position I held when I saw that we were doing no good, while we were exposing good men to great risks.

Another reason I had for my determination to retire from the I.R. B. was – circumstances brought to my knowledge *the fact* that an alarming condition of things had manifested itself in several places. Men of good records were becoming demoralised, some to whose custody money had been entrusted committed breach of trust. Even robberies had been planned by some daring men who gave out that their object was to get money for the Organisation. This I considered it my duty to denounce and I issued a private note for circulation among the men of the Organisation. On this occasion also I was threatened – whether by the same men I do not remember.

Having made up my mind that no good could be done by the IRB organisation under conditions then prevailing I decided that I should withdraw from it.

I had for some years occupied a prominent position in the organisation and at meetings at which I had occasion to meet other prominent men I felt compelled to complain of the action of some of my colleagues – by whom conduct subversive to the discipline required by our rulers was supported; and, on two occasions I think, I stated that I could not consent to such conduct and unless the gentleman who supported it withdrew that support, I could be no party to the meeting at which his views were accepted or not condemned.

On those occasions I did not receive what I could consider adequate support for my views. This also helped to induce me to retire from a position which I considered I could no longer occupy with benefit to the cause or without doing violence to my notions of right and proper.

And the time having come for again meeting my colleagues I went with the determination to withdraw. I met two of them and having told them that I had decided to withdraw and take no further part in the proceedings, I remarked that – I feared I should have to blame myself for having been to some extent responsible for having brought forward a man who I thought like to prove a dangerous man. To my astonishment the countenance of one of the two underwent an extraordinary change; I never saw anything like it – he actually became green in the face, from which he appeared to take my remark as intended for himself. Which was not at all the case. I had had nothing to do in bring *him* forward, and was well able to do so. However, he whom I meant did subsequently play a dangerous part. And in my opinion the other gentleman also had since played a bad part but not attended with danger to himself.

I therefore went to Dublin to meet my colleagues to acquaint them with my intention to resign my position. When my friends in Cork learned what I had done, the very men who not long before upbraided me with my rashness in still carrying on the work took a very curious turn. They decided that I should not be allowed to withdraw from the Organisation; two of them drive to my house (I was then living on Blackrock Road, Rose Cottage). But I met them on the way – they said they were deputed to tell me that I would not be allowed to retire. This was of course a menace. The idea that those men thought I could be influenced by threats offended me but of course I despised the menace. I did not give them much chance for talking. Immediately that I had heard what their errand was I turned my back on them – and without a word I walked away.

Chapter 10

Conclusions

———————

I need hardly say I was not indifferent to the Home Rule Movement that had been in progress from 1870 to this time under King-Harman, Butt, Shaw and Parnell. From the beginning I had wished well to it and hoped that good might come from it; but I did not in any [*sic*] identify myself with it. Indeed I had not sufficient confidence in those at the head of it. I was also influenced by my old conviction that if anything was possible by moral force O'Connell would have accomplished it; and to expect another man greater than O'Connell in our generation was asking too much.

At the same time I was entirely friendly and I constantly defended Parnell from the fault findings of those who acknowledged him as their leader.

I think it was about 1880 I noticed in the *Cork Examiner* a letter or article imputing to Mr C. G. Doran of Queenstown and myself hostile or unfriendly feelings towards the new movement. I did not hesitate to deny this very distinctly for myself.

I was yet very slow to place trust of confidence in Parnell – I was wishing that he might turn out well – but I could not see how this young man could withdraw himself from his aristocratic surroundings and throw himself into the popular ranks.

As the years went by my doubts of Parnell weakened – for I saw he was succeeding; and by 1884 I began to wish that I might have part with those who I thought were about to win Home Rule for Ireland.

[*A Chapter Ten, 'Rest before Travail 1874–1879', describing an extended holiday in Northern France and Jersey, has been omitted here*].

Home Rule was not *all* I could wish for. I often observed the tendency in our people to strive to do in their own generation what might perhaps be better done if the work were shared with other generations. This refers to the building of churches etc in which an amazing amount has been accomplished in the past sixty years in Ireland. Nothing like it or at all approaching it had probably ever been done in any other country – especially when the poverty of Ireland is considered. I would then have been very pleased to have secure Home Rule for my country – or rather to have had even a very small part in that good work – leaving another generation of Irishmen to finish the work.

Therefore when in 1885 William O'Brien asked me whether I would be willing to join the Parliamentary Party I agreed without hesitation, and when the General Election of 1885 came Parnell proposed me as one of the Candidates for Mayo at the convention held in Castlebar – towards the end of October or early in November as well as I remember. I was adopted for South Mayo. George Orme Malley QC opposed me in the hope I believe that I was disqualified – having been convicted of high treason and that no matter how few votes he might get he could secure the seat. In this however he was entirely at fault – for I had received a free pardon. Mr Malley got 75 votes while I got over 5,000.

My first interview with Parnell was when I attended a meeting of the Parliamentary Party in Dublin before going to London to attend my first session. I do not remember the exact date of that meeting or where I had that interview with Parnell; but I think it was at the National League Room 43 O'Connell St.

Parnell did not impress me as favourably as I could have wished. I am usually much impressed by one's countenance, the eyes especially. For the cause – for Parnell – *as leader* I could do anything and everything but, personally, he did not attract me – then or any other time.

As a boy I was much disposed to hero-worship; but somehow I have become less easily satisfied and more critical and I find very few of my contemporaries worthy of worship.

I left Dublin for London early in January 1886 to attend my first session of Parliament. I joined the Irish Parliamentary Party full of expectation that Home Rule would be obtained in a year or two: if I had any idea that today (11 Oct. 1898) we should be no nearer to Home Rule – but rather – judging from appearances farther from it than we were in January '86, I do not think I should ever have been a member of Parliament.

In attending Parliament I felt as if in the camp of the enemy. Gladstone was the one Englishman in whom I trusted. And notwithstanding that, as Chancellor of the Exchequer in the early fifties, it was he who piled upon Ireland the weight of unjust and excessive taxation which has since drained and impoverished my unfortunate country to the point of exhaustion, the worst example in the history of the robbing of a very poor country by the wealthiest country in the world, yet somehow I feel coerced to say I believe he was honest and conscientious – that he did not know what consequences were to fall on Ireland from his budgets. I believe that since 1885 he did his best to make amends to Ireland. For thirty years he was a wonderful power, not in Great Britain only, but in the world. If I were an Englishman he should be my hero; but as I am an Irishman I can have no part in him; and I cannot forget the terrible wrong his fiscal policy has done my country – a wrong persisted notwithstanding that the Report of the Royal Commission has exposed it to the world. But as for the English MPs in general – I distrusted them at first and I distrust them now. Not to speak of Tories and Unionists – how many of the Liberals and Radicals really desire to do justice to Ireland?

The conversion of many who were influenced by Gladstone's magnetic power, was I fear, but skin deep. That there are some who honestly desire justice for Ireland I do not doubt; but they are few. And do we not see several who, during Gladstone's life, loudly professed the Home Rule doctrine – now turning their backs upon it. Do we not know that more of them would do the same – but then they see, what apparently the others do not see, that the policy of Home Rule for Ireland is their only stepping stone to office, emoluments and dignitaries.

About a month ago I met John Burns MP on the top of a tram car and we walked together a short time. He appeared to think that the Local Government Act had settled the Irish Question for the present, but I told him that that was not so; but that the County Councils etc would be used so as to make Home Rule inevitable. He was willing to give us Home Rule, 'but there must be an end to sops and doles.' I indignantly replied that his language was both unjust and offensive – I said if a brigand robbed me of £1,000 it would be neither sop nor dole if he returned me one pound. Mr Burns demurred to this statement of the case, and I called his attention to the Report of the Royal Commission on the Financial Relations between Ireland and Great Britain – which is practically a verdict found of the evidence of the Treasury Experts – showing that Ireland is overtaxed about 2 ¾ millions sterling – and that overtaxation began in 1853. He kicked hard against this – and I said England is the robber nation of the world – you have your hand in poor Ireland's pocket and you will continue robbing us as long as you can. This was too much for him and he spoke in an aggrieved tone – then I asked him – what about the war against China to compel her to buy opium from you? He appeared to be more ashamed of that than of the robbery of Ireland – and the end of our talk was – John Burns was willing to concede Home Rule to Ireland – with an Executive responsible to the Irish Parliament and with full control of her own taxation.

Now even amongst Radical Home Rulers John Burns is one of the fairest towards Ireland.

I am amazed to find that in two steps – Gladstone and John Burns – I have travelled from January 1886 to September 1898.

I had been only a few days attending when Joe Biggar instructed me to get an account book – with a Chubbs lock. In this book I entered all the monies received for the Parliamentary Fund – from Ireland, Great Britain, America, Australia. In the same book I kept account of the disposal of those sums – Up to the present I have continued to perform this duty for the Irish Parliamentary Party. Biggar was one of the Treasurers, and on his death Parnell selected me to succeed him in that Office – a position which I still occupy.

At the time that I joined the Party Parnell had already held a position of practically undisputed mastery over it. His will was the law of the Party. I have never heard how he gained such a position. Indeed, till this moment, it did not occur to me how interesting it would be to learn it. To prove that he was the right man for the position it is enough to refer to the speech of the marquis of Salisbury at Newport (Mon)[1] in October

1885; and to Gladstone's Home Rule Bills in 1886 and 1893. And I firmly believe we should have obtained Home Rule ere this if the Irish Party had not been disrupted at the end of 1890.

It is very singular that while Irishmen are generally allowed to be disposed to and fitted for good fellowship and camaraderie, there was nothing of this among the members of the Irish Party. Some of us noticed this with regret and an effort was made to bring the men together in social intercourse. Parnell however did not approve of this and of course it fell through. His reason for this attitude I never heard. Possibly he thought his hold on the Party would be greater so long as it would be composed of atoms which had no mutual attraction and no power of cohesion. It is not unlikely that if they were accustomed to meet socially cabals [*sic?*] might be formed as an outcome such meeting [*sic*]. On the other hand, I believe that if we were accustomed to meet in friendly, social gatherings, we would have got to know and respect each other and the tone of the Party would thereby be greatly improved.

It was under such an impression some of us subsequent to 1890 endeavoured to put into effect the old idea of bringing the men and their families together in social gatherings. But those who were disposed to form cabals were opposed to it and again the project failed. So that those inclined to cabal and those who would prevent cabals were equally opposed to good-fellowship and comradeship among the members of the Irish Party. And while a few are accustomed to foregather in the smoke-room over a glass and a pipe or cigar the most of us have been practically strangers to each other all those years.

I believe – indeed I am quite certain, that the result of this has been decidedly bad for the individual members and for the Party.

I was astonished when Biggar became a member of the National Liberal Club and approved of other joining it. I was also surprised that Parnell countenanced it – at least so far as not to disapprove of it. I don't know if he frequented it himself. I always thought it wrong for members of the Irish Party to identify themselves with an English party, to the extent of becoming members of the National Liberal Club, the centre and focus of the Liberal Party. From what I have heard from time to time I do not think the connection has been an advantage to the Irish MPs.

But as I have no personal knowledge of the matters talked of I shall not pursue the subject further.

During my first session or two I diligently collected cuttings of important speeches for future use; but I soon found that other members of our Party would say vastly better everything I could think ought be said. Moreover the Rules were soon so altered as to limit the opportunities for speaking, and it of course became necessary that our best men should enjoy those opportunities. Further I was, in the second year I think, appointed Treasurer of the Irish National League of Great Britain. And from that time to the present I have given much time and attention to that very important Organisation. In fact in the division of labour I was getting a fair share of the work, and I settled down to my work recognising that if I was not useful as a speaker in the House I was nevertheless useful in other ways. It is doubtful that I could [end of narrative].

Notes

Introduction

1 As described by Patrick Maume, *The Long Gestation: Irish Nationalist Life, 1891–1918* (Dublin: Gill and Macmillan, 1999), p. 74. Some records of O'Brien's various treasury duties are held in the National Library of Ireland, Mss 9222–9225, 9232–9236.

2 See R. V. Comerford, *The Fenians in Context: Irish Politics and Society 1848–82*, 2nd edn (Dublin: Wolfhound Press, 1998). Excerpts from O'Brien's memoir have been published: Pat McCarthy, 'James Francis Xavier O'Brien (1828–1905): Dungarvan-born fenian', *Decies*, 54 (1998), pp. 107–38. McCarthy's article has informed two recent studies of Fenianism: Marta Ramón, *A Provisional Dictator: James Stephens and the Fenian Movement* (Dublin: UCD Press, 2007) and Owen McGee, *The IRB: the Irish Republican Brotherhood from the Land League to Sinn Féin* (Dublin: Four Courts, 2005).

3 See in particular Mary Louise Pratt, *Imperial Eyes: Travel Writing and Transculturation* (London and New York: Routledge, 1992).

4 The term is Comerford's; he mentions John O'Leary, John Devoy, Michael Davitt, Joseph Denieffe and Jeremiah O'Donovan Rossa as being such figures. Comerford, *Fenians in Context*, p. 7.

5 On Webb see Jennifer Regan-Lefebvre, *Cosmopolitan Nationalism in the Victorian Empire: Ireland, India and the Politics of Alfred Webb* (Basingtoke: Palgrave, 2009).

6 Webb to J. F. X. O'Brien, 10 Oct. 1898 (NLI, J. F. X. O'Brien papers, MS 16,696).

7 Repeal was shorthand for 'repeal of the Act of Union', 1801 legislation that had made Ireland an integral part of the United Kingdom, with parliamentary representation at Westminster. Repealers wished to see this legislation overturned and, by implication, the establishment of an independent Irish parliament in Dublin.

8 Christine Kinealy, *The Great Irish Famine: Impact, Ideology and Rebellion* (Basingstoke: Palgrave, 2002), p. 72.

9 The food exported would have been insufficient anyway, and government attitudes towards relief and trade were complex. See, for example, Peter Solar, 'The Great Famine was no ordinary subsistence crisis', in E. Margaret Crawford (ed.), *Famine: the Irish Experience* (Edinburgh: John Donald, 1989); Peter Gray, *Famine, Land, and Politics: British Government and Irish Society, 1843–50* (Dublin: Irish Academic Press, 1999); Cormac Ó Gráda, *Black '47 and Beyond: The Great Irish Famine in History, Economy and Memory* (Princeton: Princeton University Press, 1999).

10 Ramón, *A Provisional Dictator*, p. 58.

11 Siân Reynolds, 'Running away to Paris: expatriate women artists of the 1900 generation, from Scotland and points south', *Women's History Review*, IX: 2 (2000), p. 329.

12 Heffernan is discussed in Nicholas Daly, 'The woman in white: Whistler, Heffernan, Courbet, Du Maurier', *Modernism/Modernity*, XII: 1 (January 2005), pp. 1–25.

13 Reynolds, 'Running away to Paris', p. 330.

14 Lawrence A. Clayton, 'The Nicaragua Canal in the nineteenth century: prelude to American Empire in the Caribbean', *Journal of Latin American Studies*, 19: 2 (November 1987), pp. 323–52.

15 R. L. Woodward, 'Central America', in Leslie Bethell (ed.), *Spanish American after Independence, c.1820–1870* (Cambridge, 1987), pp. 192–3, 200–1.

16 'Position of General Walker in Nicaragua', *Freeman's Journal* (16 April 1856).

17 'Latest intelligence', *Belfast News-letter* (1 April 1856).

18 Flora Annie Steel, *The Complete Indian Housekeeper and Cook* (1888), in Antoinette Burton (ed.), *Politics and Empire in Victorian Britain: A Reader* (Basingstoke: Palgrave, 2001).

19 See Jennifer M. Regan, '"We could be of service to other suffering people": representations of India in the Irish nationalist press, c.1857–1887', *Victorian Periodicals Review*, 41: 1 (Spring 2008), pp. 61–77; Julie M. Dugger, 'Black Ireland's race: Thomas Carlyle and the Young Ireland Movement', *Victorian Studies*, 48: 3 (Spring 2006), pp. 461–85.

20 Mitchel's position has been recently and neatly summarised in James Quinn, 'Southern citizen: John Mitchel, the Confederacy and slavery', *History Ireland*, 15: 3, 'Ireland and Slavery' (May–June 2007), pp. 30–5, esp. p. 31. See also James Quinn, *John Mitchel* (Dublin: UCD Press, 2008); John Mitchel, *The Last Conquest of Ireland (Perhaps)*, ed. Patrick Maume (Dublin: UCD Press, 2005).

21 Robert C. Reinders, 'Militia in New Orleans, 1853–1861', *Louisiana History*, 3: 1 (Winter 1962), pp. 33–42, p. 37.

22 Eric Arnesen, *Waterfront Workers of New Orleans: Race, Class, and Politics, 1863–1923* (Oxford: Oxford University Press, 1991), pp. 4–5.

23 'The Fenian Rising', *Bristol Mercury*, 16 Mar. 1867.

24 *Freeman's Journal and Daily Commercial Advertiser* (29 May 1867).

25 On different classes of prison see Victor Bailey, 'Introduction', in Victor Bailey (ed.), *Policing and Punishment in Nineteenth Century Britain* (London: Croom Helm, 1981), pp. 16–19.

26 Seán McConville, *Irish Political Prisoners 1848–1922: Theatres of War* (Abingdon, UK: Routledge, 2003), p. 171.

27 John Martin to Butt, 20 May [1870?] (NLI, Butt papers, MS 8692/7).

28 For recent scholarship on the New Departure and its effect on Parnellite and post-Parnellite politics, see James McConnel, '"Fenians at Westminster": The Edwardian Irish Parliamentary Party and the legacy of the New Departure', *Irish Historical Studies*, 34: 133 (May 2004), pp. 42–64; Matthew Kelly, '"Parnell's Old Brigade": The Redmondite-Fenian nexus in the 1890s', *Irish Historical Studies*, 33: 130 (November 2002), pp. 209–32; Patrick Maume, 'Parnell and the IRB Oath', *Irish Historical Studies*, 29: 115 (May 1995), pp. 363–70.

29 For more detail see Regan-Lefebvre, *Cosmopolitan Nationalism*, pp. 106–14.

30 O'Brien's position is described in F. S. L. Lyons, *The Fall of Parnell, 1890–91* (London: Routledge and Kegan Paul, 1960), pp. 121, 134, 149.

Chapter 1 [Early Years in Waterford]

1 James Vincent Cleary, Roman Catholic Archbishop of Kingston, Canada, was born in Dungarvan in 1828. He was best known as a fierce supporter of separate education for Canadian Catholics. His death was reported in the *Freeman's Journal* (25 February 1898).

2 William Smith O'Brien (1803–64) was an Irish repealer and MP. He led the Young Ireland rebellion in 1848 and was arrested and transported to Tasmania. His sentence was overturned in 1854.

3 The O'Brien family were kings of Thomond and a powerful Gaelic family in Munster up until the eighteenth century. After the Williamite wars a branch of the family joined the established Church of Ireland.

4 To 'mitch' is to be truant.

5 Theobold Mathew (1790–1856) was a Capuchin priest who led a national temperance campaign in Ireland between 1839 and 1842. If O'Brien was born in 1831, he may have met Mathew when he was eight or nine. See Colm

Kerrigan, 'Mathew, Theobald (1790–1856)', *Oxford Dictionary of National Biography* (Oxford: Oxford University Press, 2004), or E. Malcolm, *'Ireland Sober, Ireland Free': Drink and Temperance in Nineteenth-Century Ireland* (Dublin: Gill and Macmillan, 1986).

6   I have been unable to locate a copy of 'Adventures of Captain Freeny', which apparently provided inspiration for Thackeray. See Robert A. Colby, 'Barry Lyndon and the Irish hero', *Nineteenth-Century Fiction*, 21: 2 (September 1966), pp. 109–30.

7   William Harcourt (1827–1904) was a Liberal MP who held several important government positions, including Chancellor of the Exchequer twice. He favoured regressive taxation and also introduced the inheritance tax. See Peter Stansky, 'Harcourt, Sir William George Granville Venables Vernon (1827–1904)', *ODNB*, or Martin J. Daunton, 'The political economy of death duties: Harcourt's Budget of 1894', in N. B. Harte and Roland Edwin Quinault (eds), *Land and society in Britain, 1700–1914* (Manchester: Manchester University Press, 1996), pp. 137–71.

8   The Battle of Ventry Harbour was a battle between Dara Down (or Donn) and Finn MacCool. Many versions were published in the nineteenth century, one of the better-known being John Hawkins Simpson, *Poems of Oisin, Bard of Erin, or 'The battle of Ventry harbour,' etc, from the Irish* (Dublin: McGlashan and Gill, 1857).

9   John O'Leary (1830–1907) was an Irish nationalist who edited the suppressed Fenian newspaper, the *Irish People*. He served six years in prison for treason. See Alan O'Day, 'O'Leary, John (1830–1907)', *ODNB*.

10   Ballingarry is a Tipperary town and site of conflict during the 1848 Rising.

11   Repeal refers to the repeal of the Act of Union between Great Britain and Ireland and the reestablishment of an independent parliament in Dublin. The Repeal movement was led by the Irish MP Daniel O'Connell (1775–1847) from 1830 until 1847.

12   Shoneen: from the Irish *seoinín*. A person who puts on airs, often used to suggest someone who affects Englishness.

13   Daniel O'Connell was imprisoned on this date for conspiracy. In 1843 the government decided to suppress O'Connell's final 'monster meeting' in Clontarf, north Dublin, and O'Connell agreed to cancel the meeting as a show of his support for the law; some followers saw his concession as a defeat. He was arrested for conspiracy but not detained long.

14   Members of the Young Ireland movement, a romantic nationalist movement that began in sympathy with the Repeal Movement but subsequently split

from it. Young Ireland published the newspaper and literary magazine *The Nation* and led a botched rising in 1848. Thomas Davis (1814–45) was a journalist and poet. Charles Gavan Duffy (1816–1903) edited *The Nation* but later emigrated to Australia, where he enjoyed a political and literary career.

15 'd' is the shorthand for a penny. There were 20 shillings in a pound and 12 pence in a shilling. For context, D'Arcy has estimated that Dublin general labourers' wages ranged between 16 and 20 pence per day for the period 1830–52. Fergus A. D'Arcy, 'Wages of labourers in the Dublin building industry, 1667–1918', *Saothar*, XIV (1989), p. 23, table 6.

16 Public workhouses were established under the Poor Law of 1838. They were designed to be unpleasant as a deterrent. For a recent history of the Poor Law see Peter Gray, *The Making of the Irish Poor Law, 1815–43* (Manchester: Manchester University Press, 2009).

17 Webb crossed out the last two sentences in this paragraph regarding Indian meal.

18 Culm: waste coal.

19 Webb has written, 'Somewhat later'. Richard Lalor Sheil (1791–1851), Irish MP for Dungarvan, was master of the Royal Mint before being appointed to Florence in 1850. Brian Jenkins, 'Sheil, Richard Lalor (1791–1851)', *ODNB*. O'Day and Fleming record that he held the Dungarvan seat 1841–51. Alan O'Day and Neil Fleming, *The Longman Handbook of Modern Irish History Since 1800* (Harlow: Pearson Longman, 2005), p. 172.

20 John Francis Maguire (1815–72), founder of the O'Connellite newspaper the *Cork Examiner*. See David Steele, 'Maguire, John Francis (1815–1872)', *ODNB*.

21 A William Ponsonby held a seat in nearby Youghal in 1847. J. F. Maguire held Dungarvan in 1847, 1851, and 1852–65. O'Day and Fleming, *Longman Handbook*, pp. 159, 168.

22 The secret ballot was introduced in 1872.

23 John O'Mahony (1815–77), founder of the Irish Republican Brotherhood (Fenian movement). Like O'Brien, O'Mahony had joined a regiment in the American Civil War but never saw battle.

24 James Fintan Lalor (1807–49), Irish nationalist who planned an 1849 rebellion and contributed to the *Irish Felon* newspaper. Mary E. Daly, 'James Fintan Lalor (1807–1849) and rural revolution', in Ciaran Brady (ed.), *Worsted in the Game: Losers in Irish History* (Dublin: Lilliput Press, 1989), pp. 111–19.

25 Thomas Clark Luby (1822–1901), follower of Lalor and Fenian, arrested in 1865 for his involvement with the *Irish People* newspaper. Brian Griffin, 'Luby, Thomas Clarke (1822–1901)', *ODNB*.

26 John Mitchel (1815–75) was a member of Young Ireland and was deported on treason-felony charges in 1848. He escaped to America, settled in Tennessee, and become a strong supporter of the American southern states and the institution of slavery.

27 Dominic O'Brien (1798–1873) was made bishop of Waterford and Lismore in 1855. He signed the 'Address of the Roman Catholic Bishop and Clergy of Waterford to the Queen, in Favour of Self-Government', *Freeman's Journal* (12 May 1848).

Chapter 2 Medicine Studies in Galway and Paris

1 Grinder: a tutor.

2 Webb has crossed out this paragraph and written in the margin, 'This is not worth recording and in spite of what you have said on previous page would give an incorrect impression of the general tenor of your life in Galway.'

3 Webb has crossed out this paragraph and written in the margin, 'I would leave this incident out. It gives an uneccesarily unfavourable impression of Father D. The next is [illegible] and bears recording.'

4 He is discussed in Timothy Collins, 'Melville, Hart, and Anderson: early teachers of natural history, 1849–1914', in Tadhg Foley (ed.), *From Queen's College to National University: Essays on the Academic History of QCG/UCG/NUI, Galway* (Dublin: Four Courts, 1999).

5 There were several reported sightings of a 'comet' in Ireland in 1856; this comet had been predicted and the probable date of its appearance discussed in newspapers. 'Talk of the week', *The Nation* (August 1856); 'The comet', *The Nation*, 6 Sept. 1856; 'Answers to correspondents', *The Nation* (14 March 1857). Astronomers have not confirmed a comet in this year. A fireball sighting in August 1856 in Portsmouth is listed in R. P. Greg, *A Catalogue of Meteorites and Fireballs, from AD 2 to AD 1860* (London: John Murray, 1861). The event could have been a meteor, fireball or unusual lightning bolt. My thanks are due to Patrick McCafferty for his expertise on this issue.

6 Webb has written in margin, 'I would suggest the substitution of annexed page for this. As a rule it is better not unless necessary to refer so pointedly to such differences in religion. If you were writing John O'Leary's life it would be another question.'

7 John Hogan (1800–58), an Irish sculptor of religious and national art. John Turpin, 'Hogan, John (1800–1858)', *ODNB*. On the Paris Exhibition see Frank Anderson Trapp, 'The Universal Exhibition of 1855', *The Burlington Magazine*, 107: 747 (June 1965), pp. 300–5.

8 Rue Lacépède is a main road in the fifth arrondissement of Paris, the Quartier Latin.

9 Capote: in nineteenth-century French, a type of cap.

10 Faites passer: pass it along.

11 James McNeill Whistler (1834–1903) was an American-born painter. He came to France in November 1855 but was not yet a 'distinguished' painter. Joy Newton and Margaret F. MacDonald, 'Whistler: search for a European reputation', *Zeitschrift für Kunstgeschichte*, 41: 2 (1978), pp. 148–59.

12 John Martin (1812–75) was a Younger Irelander and later a Home Rule MP. Together with Kevin Izod O'Doherty (1823–1905), he was transported to Tasmania (Van Diemen's Land) for treason. O'Doherty and Martin were allowed to leave Australia in 1855 and settled in Paris. Mary Anne Kelly (1830–1910) married O'Doherty in 1855, and was a well-known nationalist poet under the pseudonym 'Eva'. Mary Helen Thuente, 'O'Doherty , Mary Anne [Eva of The Nation] (1830–1910)', *ODNB*.

13 O'Doherty was elected to North Meath in 1885. He did not stand at the next election in 1886. Alan O'Day, 'O'Doherty, Kevin Izod (1823–1905)', *ODNB*.

14 Bonne: familiar term for a maid.

15 Sir Dominick Corrigan (1802–80), Dublin physician and medical reseacher. Corrigan began by treating the Dublin poor before rising to the position of doctor to the Lord Lieutenant and many Dublin elites. L. Perry Curtis, Jr, 'Corrigan, Sir Dominic John, first baronet (1802–1880)', *ODNB*.

Chapter 3 [With William Walker in Nicaragua]

1 Walker's heroic reputation is discussed in Amy S. Greenberg, 'A gray-eyed man: character, appearance, and filibustering', *Journal of the Early Republic*, 20: 4 (Winter 2000), pp. 673–99.

2 Webb has added, 'I now regret to realise that the establishment and extension of slavery was an essential part of his policy.' O'Brien has responded in margin, 'Entirely unknown to me till this moment 19/10/98.'

3 In fact, León was a city in Nicaragua, which in 1855 had been re-declared a capital by the Liberals.

4 O'Brien appears to be using the term 'Native Americans' to refer to the long-established white, European population, as distinct from the newer European immigrant communities.

5 Walker's financing is detailed in William Oscar Scroggs, 'William Walker and the Steamship Corporation in Nicaragua', *American Historical Review*, 10: 4 (July 1905), pp. 792–811.

6   The Kossuth, a 2,000 tonne ship, left Liverpool on 10 Nov. 1856 for New Orleans under the direction of a Captain Dawson. *Liverpool Mercury* (7 November 1856).

7   There was a particularly bad outbreak in 1853. Jo Ann Carrigan, 'Yellow fever in New Orleans, 1853: abstractions and realities', *Journal of Southern History*, 25: 3 (August 1959), pp. 339–55.

8   John Savage (1828–88) did take part in the 1848 Young Ireland Rising and after emigrated to the United States, where he established himself in journalism and became proprietor of the *Washington States Journal*. D. J. O'Donoghue, 'Savage, John (1828–1888)', rev. Marie-Louise Legg, *ODNB*.

9   Richard D'Alton Williams (1822–62) was a poet who contributed to the *The Nation* and established the *Irish Tribune* with Kevin Izod O'Doherty. He emigrated to the United States in 1851, where he taught literature and practiced medicine, and married Elizabeth Connolly in 1856. Katherine Mullin, 'Williams, Richard Dalton (1822–1862)', *ODNB*.

10 Pierre Soulé (1801–70), French exile who settled in New Orleans. He served as a Democratic senator for Louisiana and US minister to Spain. He supported the American annexation of Cuba and the filibustering of Walker. For a description (albeit a dated and hagiographical one), see J. Preston Moore, 'Pierre Soule: southern expansionist and promoter', *Journal of Southern History*, 21: 2 (May 1955), pp. 203–23.

11 Webb was written in margin, 'The great Turgot died in 1781'.

12 Tincture of opium, which also contains morphine, was commonly prescribed for sleeping problems. See Virginia Berridge, 'Victorian opium eating: responses to opiate use in nineteenth-century England', *Victorian Studies*, 21: 4 (Summer 1978), pp. 437–61.

13 26 to 32 degrees celsius.

Chapter 4 In New Orleans before the War, 1857–1861

1   For more description of steamboat cargo, see Erik F. Haites and James Mak, 'Steamboating on the Mississippi, 1810–1860: a purely competitive industry', *Business History Review*, 45: 1 (Spring 1971), pp. 52–7, esp. pp. 55–6.

2   A 'crack' steamboat was a high-end, luxurious steamboat. I have been unable to find a reference to the 'Empire State' on the Mississippi. For images and further description of the interiors of luxury steamers, see Denys P. Myers, 'The architectural development of the western floating palace', *Journal of the Society of Architectural Historians*, 11: 4 (December 1952), pp. 25–31.

3   Webb has written in margin here, 'He was acquitted, took out a medical degree at Edinburgh and in 1851 emigrated to Louisiana.'

4   Thibodeauxville, also known as Thibodeaux and now Thibodaux, and Iberville are towns west of New Orleans.

5   Confitures: now usually means a fruit jam; more generally, confections.

6   Persiennes: shutters. Mary Louise Christovich and Roulhac Toledano, *New Orleans Architecture, Volume IV: The Creole Faubourgs* (Greztna, Louisiana: Pelican Publishing, 1974), p. 144.

7   Here in the manuscript there are two sets of pages numbered 94–9 – evidently Webb was in favour of scrapping most of the second set, which are descriptions of New Orleans. I have placed these first, continuing the narrative of the history of the city.

8   Tregle describes this 'lack of rigidity in such matters' as a distinctive aspect of Creole culture in ante-bellum New Orleans. Joseph G. Tregle, Jr., 'Creoles and Americans', in Arnold R. Hirsch and Joseph Logsdon, *Creole New Orleans: Race and Americanization* (Baton Rouge, 1992), p. 144.

9   Rousey finds that one-quarter of nineteenth-century police shootings were an abuse of police power, and that public confidence in the New Orleans police was low. Dennis C. Rousey, 'Cops and guns: police use of deadly force in nineteenth-century New Orleans', *American Journal of Legal History*, 28: 1 (January 1984), pp. 41–66, esp. p. 59.

10   Prunella boots were short, flat boots, normally made of leather, with an elastic side gore.

Chapter 5   In New Orleans after the War, 1861–1862

1   Here Webb has written in the margin, 'Although the first introduction of slaves was by the Dutch, England and the New England states were mainly responsible for the extension of the system.'

2   Webb's margin note: 'I suggest leaving this out. Slavery had died out in the North before the abolition movement arose about 1834.'

3   Webb wrote on accompanying page, 'I would suggest inserting something like: "I cannot but give my own impressions and conclusions at the time. They differ from many of my friends and those to whom I have shown these recollections in manuscript. I am glad to be assured that the negroes in the South are now making rapid advances in civilisation and comfort, and that the South itself is satisfied with the decontinuance of the system. The cotton crop which in 1793 was but 1250 bales of 400 lbs each, rose under the impetus of the

discoveries I have referred to 5,000 bales in 1801. By 1860 it was 5,887,000 bales. By 1870, in consequence of the war it had fallen to 3,012,000 bales. It had under freedom in 1887 (the last figures I can find) risen to 7,425,000 bales. The total value of the slaves, a 'property' recognised by the constitution of the United States, at the moderate average value of £100 each, was £400,000,000."'

4   The Louisiana Tigers was an infantry comprised of several battalions, including Major Roberdeau Wheat's Special Battalion and the Walker Guards (who had formerly served under Walker in Nicaragua). Fourteen per cent of the Tigers were Irish. Terry L. Jones, 'Wharf-Rats, cutthroats and thieves: the Louisiana Tigers, 1861–1862', *Louisiana History*, 27: 2 (Spring 1986), pp. 147–65, pp. 147, 149.

5   The Battle of Bull Run, or the Battle of Manassas, was fought in Virginia in July, 1861. It was the first major battle of the war and was considered a Confederate victory.

6   Admiral David Farragut led the Union navy's successful attack of New Orleans. General Benjamin Butler was his army counterpart, who took over the administration of the occupied city.

7   On the Confederacy's inadequacies in naval defence, see Bern Anderson, 'The naval strategy of the Civil War', *Military Affairs*, 26: 1 (Spring 1962), pp. 11–21.

Chapter 6 At Home Organising, 1862–1867

1   James Clery and Co., wholesale grocery and wine merchants, 18–19 Caroline St and 2 Sidney Place, Cork. *The City of Cork Directory* (Fulton, 1871), p. 25, digitised by Cork City Council on www.corkpastandpresent.ie.

2   O'Brien has provided a margin note here: 'In ancient Irish history are to be found full particulars of the exploits of a national militia organised and commanded by Finn MacCumhaill, and known as Fenians. John O'Mahony, one of the chief organisers of the Irish Republican Brotherhood, translated from the Irish Keating's *History of Ireland* [*History of Ireland from the earliest period to the English Invasion*, by the Reverend Geoffrey Keating, D. D. translated from the original Gaelic and copiously annotated by John O'Mahony (New York: publisher unknown, 1857)]. Hence the modern application of the term Fenian.'

3   The Church of Ireland was a state church until 1870.

4   In 1871, 96.3 per cent of County Waterford was Catholic and 3.2 per cent was Church of Ireland. Alan O'Day and Neil Fleming, *The Longman Handbook of Modern Irish History Since 1800* (Harlow: Pearson Longman, 2005), p. 460.

5   Queen's Old Castle Company was a wholesale and retail department store on Great Georges Street. *City of Cork Directory*, p. 129.

6   Rossa married Mary Jane Irwin on 22 Nov. 1864. Owen Dudley Edwards, 'Rossa, Jeremiah O'Donovan (*bap.* 1831, *d.* 1915)', *ODNB*.

7   Charles Stewart Parnell (1846–91) led the Irish Parliamentary Party in the 1880s. His fall in 1890 after being named in a divorce case involving one of his MPs led to a split in the Party, which had not been fully resolved at the time O'Brien was writing.

8   The *Freeman's Journal* reported the arrest of ten people from the *Irish People*, including Rossa and O'Connor, on 16 Febuary 1865.

9   Mourne Mountains.

10   Hugh Francis Brophy was arrested and sentenced to ten years' penal servitude in January 1866. He chose to go to Australia. *Return of Names and Sentences of Fenian Convicts proposed to be released*, 1868–69; 1869 (72), LI.531.

11   Webb has written in margin here, 'An utterly false allegation. Whatever Stephens was he was in [illegible] true to Ireland.'

12   The Parliamentary Inquiry suggested that the prison night-watchman, Daniel Byrne, was responsible. *James Stephens. Copy of the report of the inspectors general of prisons in Ireland to His Excellency the Lord Lieutenant with regard to the escape of James Stephens*, 1866 (147), LVIII.479.

13   Description used by Young Irelander Thomas Davis in his poem 'Fontenoy', of the Irish troops fighting alongside the French against the English. The Irish troops were led by an O'Brien.

Chapter 7 On the Hill-Side, 1867

1   William Mackey Lomasney was born in Ohio and died in 1883 while trying to blow up London Bridge. See Thomas N. Brown, 'The origins and character of Irish-American nationalism', *The Review of Politics*, 18: 3 (July 1956), pp. 327–58, p. 331.

2   Here Webb has inserted a note: 'I think you will find that this is all duplicate. It has already been said or will be said in following pages.' I have included it.

3   There is a Ballyknockane about six miles south of Mallow.

4   Webb has written in margin, 'a curate'.

5   Webb has written in margin surrounding this paragraph, 'Is it necessary to relate this incident so shameful to the good faith of the party?'

6   Possibly D. Canty, 3 Caroline Street, Cork. *The City of Cork Directory*, p. 258.

7   In margin: 'Arrested 7/3/67'.

8   Written in margin alongside this paragraph: 'left out or rewritten'.

9   They were John McClure, John Edward Kelly, Thomas Cullinan and David Joyce. McClure and Kelly were both described as around 22-years-old and 'very respectably dressed', whereas 'Cullinan is an able man of the peasant class, and Joyce is a person evidently of a very humble position in life'. 'Cork Special Commission', *Freeman's Journal*, (Wednesday, 22 May 1867). Regarding O'Brien's inability to remember their names, Webb has written a note, 'Look up report of Constitution and find exact particulars. Or you will find it in full of *Times* at the House [of Commons]. They are in a room near lower Smoking Room.'

10   A coastguard station near Youghal in East Cork.

Chapter 8 Trial and Imprisonment, 1867–1869

1   Denis Caulfield Heron (1824–81), lawyer, academic and Liberal MP for Tipperary, 1870–4.

2   Daniel William Cahill (1796–1864), Catholic priest, scientist and nationalist polemicist.

3   In Ireland three were sentenced to death in 1867 and four in 1866.

4   Webb was written over this, 'under middle height'.

5   The United Irishmen led an insurrection in 1798 across several regions of Ireland, including Wexford. The insurrection was suppressed and its leaders, including Wolfe Tone and Lord Edward Fitzgerald, died or were executed for their involvement.

6   A stone is 14 pounds; 9 1/2 stone is 133 pounds; 12 stone is 168 pounds, and 14 stone is 196 pounds.

7   Holyhead is a port in Wales.

8   Parliamentary reports intended it to be leftover meat in a broth, flavoured with onion and thickened with leftover bread. *Reports of Committee to inquire into Dietaries of Convict Prisons*, 1864 (467), XLIX.9.

9   Refers to the celebrated German historian: Leopold von Ranke, *The Popes of Rome: Their Ecclesiastical and Political History during the Sixteenth and Seventeenth Centuries*, Trans. Sarah Austin, 3 vols (London: John Murray, 1841).

10   Webb has written in margin, 'I suggest for reasons before given leaving this out.'

11   Webb had written in margin, 'Better out – O'Leary is alive.'

12   A paragraph here by J. F. X. that Webb has crossed out: 'It is now the 6th of October 1896 and owing to the Parliamentary Session – which began in February and ended about the middle of August – the memorable Convention

of the Irish Race held in Dublin September 1, 2 and 3 – followed by the INLGB [Irish National League of Great Britain] Convention Sept 4 – private affairs also intervening – I am only now able to resume these writings.'

Chapter 9   1869–1874

1   Gill was proprietor of the republican *Tipperary Advocate*. The *Nenagh Guardian* was a conservative publication. Alan O'Day and Neil Fleming, *The Longman Handbook of Modern Irish History Since 1800* (Harlow: Pearson Longman, 2005), pp. 384, 391.

2   Gill successfully contested Tipperary County in 1865.

3   PP is 'parish priest'.

4   Webb has noted here that Rossa was actually elected but was disqualified, and then a new election was held.

5   The Amnesty Association had campaigned to have Fenians' prison sentences commuted.

6   O'Brien is referring to Isaac Butt's Home Government Association, inaugurated in 1870, rather than the Irish Protestant Home Rule Association established in 1886.

7   Webb has written in margin, 'Not worth mentioning.'

8   Webb has written in margin, 'Omit?'

9   Michael Davitt (1846–1905), Irish nationalist MP, land reformer and labour leader. Davitt was imprisoned between 1870 and 1877 for his role in Fenian gun running. Webb has written in margin a rephrasing: 'But if they were a necessary factor in the chain of circumstances that has given him such a prominent and useful place,' followed by, 'Ask Davitt's permission to mention this.'

Chapter 10   Conclusion

1   Newport (Mon): Mon was short for Monmouthshire.

Index